Start

Rightly Dividing

. . . .

How to start studying

with the right heart

from the right Bible

rightly divided.

START

RIGHTLY DIVIDING

How to start studying
with the right heart
from the right Bible
rightly divided.

Justin Curtis Johnson
Compiled by **Jeremey Johnson**

Ambassadors
Publishing.*com*

2015

ISBN-13   978-1-942548-00-3
ISBN-10   1-942548-00-1

 Ambassadors
Publishing.*com*

P.O. Box 161
Swayzee, Indiana 46986
www.ambassadorspublishing.com

To my brother, Jeremey, who compiled this book,
and whose initiative from the beginning
helped me start rightly dividing.

About this Book

This book is a collection of writings by Justin Johnson, preacher at Grace Ambassadors Bible Fellowship in Swayzee, Indiana. The writings were originally published at GraceAmbassadors.com. Website subscribers received these weekly Bible study tips and lessons on rightly dividing the word of truth via email updates. Original writings are separated by their own title or the graphic below, in the case of longer articles. They are compiled here as a guide for learning how to study the Bible the way God intended.

CONTENTS

THE PUBLISHER'S PREFACE:
THE PREACHING OF THE CROSS

The Bible says the preaching of the cross is the power of God, the wisdom of God, and the glory of God unto salvation (1 Cor 1:18, 24; Rom 1:16; Phil 3:7-11).

By the cross, enemies are reconciled to God and have peace with him (Col 1:20; Rom 5:1; 2 Cor 5:19). The blood shed there secures forgiveness and redemption (Eph 1:7). The preaching of the cross gives eternal life to all who trust its resurrection power. By the cross, God takes ungodly sinners and freely justifies them through faith (Rom 3:24, 4:5, 5:1).

How can this be right? How can God give salvation to ungodly men by mere faith? Should not God merit salvation by good works? Would not God receive more glory by works? Abundant good works cannot justify a single sin. We are all sinners. The wages of sin is death (Rom 3:23, 6:23). A million good works amount to nothing when one sin results in death.

There is no glory in a sinner trying to impress a righteous God with his good works. It is futile. Religion does not impress God, and flattery is fake. God owes us nothing. Sin and boasting will cost you everything (1 Cor 1:29). Man cannot *earn* salvation. God can only *give* salvation. You have nothing with which to pay. He must provide salvation freely.

This is what God provided in Jesus, the one and only perfect Christ, through his blood, death, burial, and resurrection. Christ's blood is the payment, his resurrection is the receipt, and the preaching of the cross is the delivery. All that remains is for us to believe!

Christ did everything necessary to save your soul. The Lord Jesus Christ was made sin for us, abolished death with his resurrection power, and made immortality and righteousness an opportunity to all through him. This sufficient and finished work provides salvation freely to all and upon all that believe. Trust God's righteousness in Christ, not your own, and you will be saved (Rom 3:20-26).

The preaching of the cross is the power of God unto salvation. Talk of salvation is vain without it. Give glory to God for doing the needed work. Glory in the cross!

> "[Christ Jesus] Whom God hath set forth to be a propitiation through faith in his blood, to declare his righteousness for the remission of sins that are past, through the forbearance of God; To declare, I say, at this time his righteousness: that he might be just, and the justifier of him which believeth in Jesus."
>
> – Romans 3:25-26

> "But to him that worketh not, but believeth on him that justifieth the ungodly, his faith is counted for righteousness." – Romans 4:5

> "I declare unto you the gospel... by which also ye are saved... that Christ died for our sins according to the scriptures; and that he was buried, and that he rose again the third day according to the scriptures..."
>
> - 1 Corinthians 15:1-4

INTRODUCTION

The Bible is a book that needs to be studied. This is no less true knowing that most Christians barely read it. Reading gives familiarity, but study supplies understanding. The apostle Paul said, "Study to shew thyself approved unto God, a workman that needeth not to be ashamed…" (2 Tim 2:15). Shamefully, there are few that do the work and fewer still that understand what the Bible says. Without a doubt, the Bible needs to be studied, but how?

After visiting our church and hearing the importance of personal Bible study, people frequently ask, "How do I start?" The prospect of studying 31,102 verses and 788,280 words in the Bible can be daunting. The task is like being charged with eating an elephant. How does one eat an entire elephant? The hackneyed response is "one bite at a time." Take the large task and divide it.

The Bible is naturally divided into 66 books, but the thought of reading so many books does not make it any easier. Publishers divide the Bible into the Old and New Testaments, but this has unintentionally caused more harm than help. With genealogies, ancient history, cryptic prophecies, and Jewish traditions how do we divide the Bible to understand it clearly? More importantly, and to cut to the chase, where do we find the part of the Bible that applies to us today? How do we rightly divide the word of truth as Paul instructs in 2 Timothy 2:15?

The right place to start is by preparing our hearts and getting the right tools. Before study happens there needs to be a right heart toward the right Bible. Only then, can we start rightly dividing the word of truth and ultimately profit from finally understanding the Bible. Let's get started!

Part I

GETTING STARTED

"Let God be true, but every man a liar…"
-Romans 3:4

CHAPTER 1
BIBLE BELIEF

Before you study the Bible, you need to make a choice. You must choose whether your mind has flaws that need corrected or if God's word has flaws that need corrected.

People who choose that the Bible has flaws will accept only those parts that align with their way of thinking, serve their interests, or speak positively about their way of life. Bible believers admit that the Bible is perfect whereas they are not. This results in a change of mind that aligns with Biblical truth.

If you want to grow in the knowledge of the truth, you must start by eliminating the idea that your Bible has flaws that need corrected. You are the one that needs corrected, and that by God's word. If you cannot make this choice then you have no place studying the Bible. The Bible will be a closed book to you.

Bible believers submit to God's book; correctors of the Bible require God's words submit to them. Before you open the book, and the book opens to you, you must know your place. Choose to let God be true and his word perfect.

STARTING WITH FAITH

Many people have spent years poring over ancient documents, texts, and languages searching for indisputable evidence that the Bible is what it says it is: the word of God. After collecting piles of data and evidence, the same decision faces them. Are these God's words?

What is missing is faith in God to preserve his words. Without faith it is all meaningless (Heb 11:6). Before you begin to profit from studying the Bible, manuscript evidence, translation, or apologetics, you must first believe that God has inspired and preserved his words. Otherwise you are wasting time looking for something you do not believe exists. At least give God the benefit of the doubt, but the greater benefit is in receiving the Bible as the word of God.

Stop doubting the Bible to be true. Place your faith in God and determine to study your Bible as the words of God. Do you not see that God authored this book? Read its pages. Do you not find divine truth in the words of Jesus? Do you not believe the clear gospel that saves today?[1]

Faith in God's word is the beginning of intelligent Bible study. There is no object of faith more certain than God and his words. Without faith it is impossible to please God. Without faith you will be tortured by doubt your whole life, not because of a lack of evidences but simply because you deny them. We must have faith in the inspiration of God's word to the written page.

Yet, even inspiration falls short without the useful preservation of those words. Preservation is how divine inspiration reaches you in the here and now. God's word

---

[1] See the foreword to this book for the gospel preaching of the cross.

must be accessible to serve its purpose. A great truth that remains a mystery is not usable. It must be revealed. It must be available. It must be preserved. God has spoken plainly and directly to us through his written word. All we have to do is trust the book God authored. Trust it as having supernatural origin, soaked in divine Truth, and readily available to discover the wisdom of God. Decide now to put your faith in God, trust your Bible and cast away all doubt. Only this will allow you to pursue the truth with confidence.

GOD'S PRESERVED WORDS

I believe every word in the King James Bible on my desk. Some may find that offensive, but I believe it is more offensive to God to believe any less.

There is no good reason to doubt that God could preserve his inspired words perfectly and without error. The winds and the seas obey him. He has measured the waters in the hollow of his hand. He declares the end from the beginning, and before the world began he knew Christ would die for my sins. He put on humanity, defeated death, and will reign over the universe for eternity. His ways are perfect, and his thoughts pure. His faithfulness never ceases, and his wisdom is infinite.

It is not a hard conclusion to make that if God inspired words for the salvation of humanity that he would preserve them for those he desired to save. Sadly, there are many who find it hard to believe every word in the Bible. Others will argue at length attempting to prove the impossibility of God's preservation through supposed mistakes and errors. There should not need to be an argument on this point according to Romans 3:3-4; nevertheless, their protestations are found severely wanting: the errors simply do not exist.[2] If they have a problem with God's words, then there will be plenty of time to talk to him about it in heaven. That is, if they are able to trust his words enough to get there.

Christians ought to be preaching and teaching belief in God and His words rather than ministering doubt. What good comes from standing in doubt of the Bible when its words of life and peace work only in them that believe?[3]

There is a good reason that I believe every word in my King James Bible. The reason is that my faith in God depends upon it.[4]

"...faith cometh by hearing, and hearing by the word of God."
— Romans 10:17

I cannot know God without believing the Bible in my hands. I cannot be throughly furnished to do every good work without believing every word of the Bible on my lap.

"All scripture is given by inspiration of God, and is profitable... that the man of God may be perfect, throughly furnished unto all good works."
— 2 Timothy 3:16-17

---

[2] Commonly the supposed errors are instances of polysemy, spelling, archaic words, translation preference, and contextual contradictions, all of which are not true errors or mistakes.

[3] 1 Thess 2:13; 1 Cor 2:14

[4] Faith is born from the word of God being heard. In its beginning, faith does not require hearing every word of the Bible. Faith is conceived with only a few words, but if the man of God is to be perfect, then "all scripture" must be available and perfect (2 Tim 3:16).

Most importantly, it is an offense to my Lord if I continue in unbelief. It is not a matter of probability that God's words are preserved. Neither is it a matter of man's capability. It is a matter of God's responsibility.

"And being fully persuaded that, what he had promised, he was able also to perform." – Romans 4:21

PRESERVATION: THE BIBLE ISSUE

Sometimes people confess that they still do not understand the "Bible issue." They mean Bible translations; which one is the right one? The pivotal doctrine on this issue is not inspiration but preservation.

Bible conservatives say God's word was inspired without error *in the originals*. We do not have the originals any more, and so the original inerrancy is lost. Bible liberals say God's word was never inspired without error in the originals, and we still do not have an inerrant Bible.

Bible believers know that the issue in Bible translation is not inspiration, but preservation. Without preservation there is no such thing as an inerrant Bible on any bookshelf anywhere. Who cares if there was once an inerrant Bible lost sometime in the past? If it is impossible to have one today, it is impossible to know what it said. Has God preserved his words throughout history and languages, or not? If he has, then we should be looking for the right Bible that is accurate and inerrant in recent history. If he has not, then we can never be sure the Bible is completely without error until we find indefinitely more yet-to-be-discovered evidence.

Preservationists look for a text that has existed throughout history. Those with a weak view of preservation are inclined to believe that it has been lost and so give more weight to rare, obscure, and recent discoveries. I believe God inspired the scripture according to 2 Timothy 3:16 and perfectly preserved it to accomplish 2 Timothy 3:17 in us that believe. Once you understand preservation, there is really only one historic text that is accurate and inerrant.

GOD'S WORDS TRANSLATED

In Genesis 11:7, God confounds the language of humanity. From that point on, men who thought the same thoughts, felt the same feelings, and experienced the same world used different words to speak.

As men began to learn other languages, they could translate the words of one language into the words of another. We have been doing this for millennia. God did it supernaturally in men in Acts 2:6.

In the book of Exodus, Moses spoke Egyptian to the Pharaoh, but every written record discovered contains a translation into another language such as Hebrew. Moses translated spoken Egyptian into written Hebrew, and now we have it today printed in English as "Let my people go" (Exo 5:1). Nothing was lost in translation.

During his defense in Jerusalem, Paul spoke in the Hebrew tongue to his kinsmen while Romans ignorant of Hebrew stood by (Acts 22:1-2). Paul's spoken Hebrew words were inspired as translated Greek and then translated today into English. We have the Hebrew words Paul spoke today only because they were first translated into Greek. It is possible to preserve words through languages. If it is possible to preserve the words of mere men, how much more the pure words of God.

6

The doctrine of preservation says that God preserves his words through languages. The Bible gives testimony to this in many places. You can trust the translated words in your Bible to be God's words. The original writers did.

EVERY MAN A LIAR

How far are you willing to go to learn the truth? Would you continue if it meant learning that you are wrong? If you can do this, you are on your way.

What if learning the truth meant that your friends were wrong? We all like to think we know a little more than our friends do. This should not be too hard.

What if discovering the truth meant that what was popular and celebrity was wrong? It is possible. After all, wise men say, "What is popular is not always right." We have already established that the average Joe and his friends can be ignorant.

What if accepting the truth meant that learned scholars and doctors were also wrong? In a world where the primary tool of truth is reason, this may be more difficult to believe. However, we also know that scholars do not agree on everything. Perhaps there is room for error after all. Could it be that entire schools are wrong about what is true? Entire denominations? Entire countries?

What if knowing the truth meant that most every historically significant man, scholar, teacher, or philosopher for the past two thousand years was wrong? Would you still accept it? Would you still want to know it, knowing you would be alone?

Paul writes, "Let God be true, but every man a liar" (Romans 3:4). Apparently, if every man that ever lived was wrong, God would still be true.

Human reason can be fallacious, and experience can be deceiving, but God and his revelation are never wrong. He is not a man that he should lie and is worthy of your trust.

It would be naive to think that any church, country, preacher, or tradition has the market on truth. When we are willing to believe God before tradition or training then we are one step closer to gaining what is more valuable than both: the truth.

Thank God that not every man in history has been wrong on everything. Where men were right, God was right first, and where men were wrong, God was still right. Ignorance is curable by the truth of the Bible, but it requires letting God be true, even if it means everyone else is wrong.

BELIEVE THE BIBLE, EVEN WHEN IT IS HARD

While studying your Bible, you will find things that are hard to believe. The world doubts the accuracy of these parts of the Bible and offers excuses for God. By world, I mean the "Christian" world. You may already know of some things in the Bible that are not widely believed by the majority of Christians.

This chapter serves to encourage you to make up your mind to trust God's word as your final authority. There will be times when you are forced to choose between the Bible and competing authorities. On the one hand the Bible is right, and on the other hand academic authorities, Christian celebrities, and religious traditions are right. Settle it in your mind now what is your final authority.

In order to be the pillar and the ground of the truth, you will need a true Bible. Choose now to trust your Bible as God's word completely. It will help your Bible study tremendously. The first line of defense against Bible confusion is to trust God's word to be without mistake. Let men make the mistakes.

Let God be true.

CHAPTER 2

HELPFUL STUDY TOOLS

Christian publishers provide a surplus of products to help with Bible study. Inexperienced Bible students can easily waste time and money buying unnecessary tools that slow down or hinder personal Bible study. This chapter will cut through the commercial confusion for those looking for the tools to get started in personal Bible study.

This list is the result of many people asking me what I use in study for sermon preparation. Though I am not an expert on every resource, these simple trusted tools work when used the right way. There are many tools in my office that are rarely used, or not worth the money, but the items below are used every time I study:

1. Bible
2. Concordance
3. Dictionary
4. Notepad
5. Software (optional)

The list may seem simple at first, but it is the place to start and will serve you well the rest of your life.

TOOL #1: BIBLE

If you can afford no other book, spend your money on a good Bible. The Bible instructs us to study to show ourselves approved unto God, and that scripture is profitable for furnishing men of God to be unashamed workmen (2 Tim 2:15; 2 Tim 3:16). It is important, then, which Bible you use as there are many different options. I believe every word of the King James Bible on my desk, and would encourage you to as well. Depending on which desk I use, the Bible on my desk is one of the following:

Church – KJV mid-size large print 215 series[1]
Hendrickson – KJV large print wide margin[2]
Cambridge – KJV Concord wide margin[3]

My Bibles are published with no notes, no references, no red letters (unless I put them there), and I like it that way. When I pick up the Bible, it is only God's words without affectation.

A NOTE ON STUDY BIBLES

Study Bibles include commentary alongside the Bible text. They are not essential for personal Bible study. I have study Bibles but do not use them as my primary Bible. They are regarded the same as commentaries in my library as I

---

[1] The regular text is the Cambridge text. Their Bibles labeled "Classic" is the Oxford text. (www.localchurchbiblepublishers.com)
[2] This Bible has some capitalization problems that separate it from the Cambridge edition text. (http://www.hendrickson.com/)
[3] This Bible has print smaller than the other two on the list, which is smaller than I like. (http://www.cambridge.org/bibles).

find the notes too distracting when reading the Bible. The only reason I have them is to get the unique perspective of the author from his notes, but stealing someone else's notes is not personal Bible study. Not to mention I do not feel comfortable carrying around someone else's thoughts and calling it my Bible.

If I was granted a wish by the publishing wizards of study Bibles, they would publish the notes separately to preserve the integrity of the scripture, save me money, and save my time flipping pages.

TOOL #2: EXHAUSTIVE CONCORDANCE

The most important tool in personal Bible study is a concordance. It is second only to your Bible. To get the most profit from it, your concordance must be exhaustive (it contains every word and every location of each word). I use the search program in my Bible software for this function, but I also have the only print concordance you will ever need: *Strong's Exhaustive Concordance* by James Strong.[4]

A concordance's strength is in making connections with other passages of the Bible. There are also various books and Bibles that give cross-references in attempt to make similar connections. All cross-references are interpretive and deserve due caution when provided from a third party. However, the best of these books is *The Treasury of Scriptural Knowledge*.[5]

---

[4] Concordances are specific to the Bible translation, so make sure you get the old Strong's which is only for the KJV. There are newer knockoffs called Strong's but are for other translations. Also, beware of the newer ringers claiming to be stronger and more complete. Exhaustive is as complete as you can get. Mine is published by Hendrickson publishers.
[5] TSK (Treasury of Scriptural Knowledge) is available for free online, and in print by Hendrickson Publishers P.O Box 3473, Peabody, MA 01961

TOOL #3: DICTIONARY

The Bible is its own best dictionary. With a Bible and a concordance you can create definitions better than most dictionaries and more descriptive of their Bible usage. Dictionaries of English can assist in defining some of the lesser used words in the Bible. An older dictionary is better only because it gives you a meaning closer to when the Bible was first published.[6]

If you cannot purchase the 1828 Webster's dictionary, there are free versions of many dictionaries online along with Webster's multiple editions.

Archaic Words in the Authorized Version by Laurence Vance is also helpful at defining words that have changed meaning in popular usage.[7]

A NOTE ON BIBLE DICTIONARIES

A Bible dictionary can help you with describing people, places, and things from the Bible with information that may not be found in the Bible. They are often equivalent to Bible notes and book prefaces in some editions of the Bible. They are treated as commentaries in my library since the content is not inspired and subject to change as new research is done.

---

[6] The King James Bible was translated in 1611, but has had several editions. The most common standards are the Oxford from Blayney's 1769 edition and the Cambridge printing circa 1900. English dictionaries were not printed until after the King James Bible.

[7] Vance Publications, P.O. Box 780671, Orlando, FL 32879 [www.vancepublications.com]

TOOL #4: NOTEPAD/JOURNAL

You cannot study the Bible without taking notes and writing down your thoughts. Invest in some notepads, blank journals, and comfortable pens or pencils. Do not be cautious with your writing at first. Write down your thoughts about the Bible and any verse references that come to mind. This is where personal Bible study happens, and it is different than hijacking someone else's meditations.

Computers may be reducing the need for paper, but paper is still very useful and less distracting than a computer. There are papers all over my computer desk with drawings, arrows, and charts drawn on them from my Bible study. Draw out your ideas and let your eyes help your brain make connections and outlines. There is still no easier way to do this than with paper and pen.

TOOL #5: BIBLE SOFTWARE (OPTIONAL)

Software can contain all of the tools listed above in one place. You can start studying the Bible with one click. The search capabilities in my software replace my printed concordance on most occasions. Software has the ability to make notes and record my cross-references. This replaces my notepads, pencils, and journals (though not completely). There are many pages of study notes on my computer with backups in case of disaster. I use Bible software extensively in my personal Bible study out of preference, but the same study results can be achieved without the use of software.

Free and inexpensive study software such as TheWord, eSword, or SwordSearcher possess all that you will ever need from Bible software.[8] Free software is open on my computer every day customized with a King James Bible, search function, dictionary, and notes readily available.

Expensive software like Logos and BibleWorks bring additional features useful for studying other languages, but study of other languages is not Bible study. They are unnecessary for personal Bible believing study in English. The most profitable features are also found in the cheaper alternatives. Save your money.

A NOTE ON COMMENTARIES & SOFTWARE

Commentaries are the product of someone else's Bible study. Since many people never start studying the Bible, the only Bible they hear is from preaching, teaching, Christian books, and commentaries. These resources are very helpful for Christians who think that facing the Bible alone is overwhelming. When the best commentaries were popular, Biblical virtues abounded. This type of literature can be extremely helpful to teach and encourage when the doctrine is right, but when the doctrine is wrong extensive damage can be done, especially if it is a substitute for personal Bible study.

This is why study of commentaries and Christian books should not be confused with personal Bible study. Just because you listen to commentary and read Christian books does not mean you know the Bible. There are important lessons that can only be learned by personally digging into God's word and thinking about it. Commentary study is not your Bible study.

---

[8] The Word [www.theword.net]; eSword [www.e-sword.net]; SwordSearcher [www.swordsearcher.com].

Teachers never have enough time to expound everything they learned in preparation and would admit that they learn more in preparation than is ever presented. Just because your teacher knows and teaches something does not mean you know it just as well. Study it on your own to teach yourself.

Commentaries are profitable, but only when studying someone else's perspective on the Bible. Use with discretion only after you have studied the Bible, understanding the commentary's doctrinal bias, and knowing that what you are reading is not the infallible word of God.

EXPENSIVE LIBRARIES AND SOFTWARE

Sometimes people ask me about spending lots of money on expensive Bible software and libraries. My answer is, "I try to avoid it." Not because I do not want to invest in good tools, but because I spot a racket when I see one. Many good classic books worth knowing well are freely available online. The most expensive books (typically written by seminary professors) often do not contain the gems it costs to purchase them. I have seen it with my own tired eyes.

Better than owning many books and knowing none of them very well, own fewer books and master their content. Better to read the books you own instead of owning more books than you can read. Better to pay less for great books than to pay more for the newest books.

Read your books. Study the good ones. Start with the Bible. You do not need thousands of books or books worth a thousand dollars to grow in God's word. You should be willing to put your money where your mouth is and invest in proper tools, but Christian literature is one place where a higher price does not always indicate higher quality. Beware.

COMMENTARIES ARE BIASED

Commentaries are good for seeing what other great thinkers thought about the scripture. However, there is a warning: they are all biased. The bias is a product of their doctrinal orientation. Writing your own commentary will have *your* own bias. Identify their bias before you start to read. Who wrote the commentary? With what denomination or church were they joined? What did they believe about the gospel?

Use a commentary only after you have already studied the passage from the Bible and have come to your own conclusion – even if it is a list of different conclusions. Sometimes commentaries can give you an idea of how far off you are. Other times you will realize the writer of the commentary had just as much trouble as you.

Commentaries are useful, but they are not scripture. They are fallible. Commentaries should be used as a reference for what a good mind or denomination concludes. They should not be your first step to doctrinal answers. The first step is getting you started studying the Bible.

GETTING STARTED...

Bible study starts with your mind in the Bible and in prayer, submitting to God and his words. The list of resources in this chapter is short for a reason. Tools are helpful, but can quickly turn into a distraction as people spend more time comparing, buying, and researching tools than they spend in the Bible. Using tools and aids can easily replace Bible study and keep you from truly profiting as you should. A short list of faithful tools is enough to get started. Getting started with Bible study requires only a Bible and a mind willing to submit to what it says.

CHAPTER 3
YOU CAN DO IT

The Bible was not written to be hidden in backwoods monasteries. It was written to be read by the poorest widow in Israel, heathen Gentiles, children, and slaves. It was not written with the lofty wisdom of the world, but with the clear language of the truth.

With the inordinate attention given to institutions offering advanced degrees, there is a tendency to think that the Bible should be left to the hands of experts. Yet, the experts repeatedly prove that they have been educated to doubt the Bible. My favorite example is the story of an oceanographer who suggested that Jesus walked on ice instead of water.[1] Ice is water, technically. Give me a break.

The Bible does not require an expert in oceanography to interpret it. If Jesus walked on ice, then it was not a miracle, and the proclamation of Matthew 14:33 would be ludicrous. Someone is a fool, and it is either the eyewitness fishermen in the boat or an expert oceanographer removed by two thousand years. I will stand with the lowly fishermen over the experts.

"Professing themselves to be wise, they became fools..."
– Romans 1:22

---

[1] Nof, Doron. "Is There A Paleolimnological Explanation for 'Walking on Water' in the Sea of Galilee?" *Journal of Paleolimnology* (2006) 35:417–439

"... your faith should not stand in the wisdom of men, but in the power of God. "   – 1 Corinthians 2:5

YOU DO NOT NEED A PH.D.

You have the words inspired by the mouth of God on your bed stand. You do not need a Ph.D. to read and understand your Bible. Right division is proof of this. When you learn how to rightly divide, people think you went to seminary. Instead, you simply understand the Bible as it was intended. He inspired it for your everyday use, not for archiving in a museum or to have its word-forms catalogued for linguistics departments worldwide.

The best and most important use of the Bible is when you pick it up to understand its teachings about God, the world, and salvation. This seems to be lost in the halls of academia. Mere Bible belief is foolish to the "scholar" who must confirm, verify, and explain away its truths with their own libraries of knowledge.

"But we preach Christ crucified, unto the Jews a stumblingblock, and unto the Greeks foolishness;"
                        – 1 Corinthians 1:23

We need more of Tyndale's ploughboys to respond to the strained doctrine of the scholars.[2]

---

[2] *"Not long after, Master Tyndale happened to be in the company of a certain divine, recounted for a learned man, and, in communing and disputing with him, he drove him to that issue, that the said great doctor burst out into these blasphemous words, "We were better to be without God's laws than the pope's." Master Tyndale, hearing this, full of godly zeal, and not bearing that blasphemous saying, replied, "I defy the pope, and all his laws;" and added, "If God spared him life, ere*

YOU CAN COMPREHEND

Holding a perfectly preserved copy of God's words, we are in the position to study for ourselves. Gone are the days when it was illegal to read the Bible and its words could only be spoken in another language by a priest class.

Nothing separates you from attaining God's wisdom except a little bit of work (2 Tim 2:15). An ounce of faith and God's words are worth more than a thousand degrees of authority. Do not ever let a scholar or self-proclaimed expert stand in the way of your faith in the Bible. They have no more authority than truth gives them.

THEOLOGY VS. BIBLE STUDY

Many people think study of theology is study of the Bible, but they are often different. Do not be fooled. The pursuit of theology has caused many in the church to become followers of theologians and theological systems instead of students of God's word. Out of fear of sounding too preachy, dogmatic, or like one of those "Bible nuts" that quotes scripture, theology is used as the tool of choice to address problems in and out of the church.

Replacing the Bible with Theological Studies replaces the pillar of the truth with ivory towers and the ground of the truth with the sacred ground of seminaries. As a result, for

many years he would cause a boy that driveth the plough to know more of the Scripture than he did." Fox's Book of Martyrs, chapter 12. [http://www.ccel.org/f/foxe/martyrs/fox112.htm]

many, the Bible is a closed book. They are told it should not be understood except by the theologically trained, ordained, and accredited.

Theologians pride themselves in their knowledge of philosophy, religious traditions, and the opinions of other theologians.

> "Beware lest any man spoil you through philosophy and vain deceit, after the tradition of men, after the rudiments of the world, and not after Christ."
>
> – Colossians 2:8

The Bible was not given for theologians. It was given for *every* man to understand. It does not require the wisdom of the world, but it does require we study it.

THE DIFFERENCE

There is a difference between studying theology and studying the Bible:

Theology asks questions like, "Does God exist?"

The Bible says, "In the beginning God created the heaven and the earth," and never questions God after that (Gen 1:1).

_____

Theology wonders, "If God intervenes, then why is there evil in the world?"

The Bible says that by one man sin entered, and that God manifest in the flesh commended his love toward us by dying for our sins (Rom 5:8-12).

Theology rhetorically states, "What is truth?"

The Bible quotes Jesus as saying, "I am the way, the truth, and the life: no man cometh unto the Father, but by me" (John 14:6).

Theology raises uncertainties and studies them.

The Bible makes us certain: "That I might make thee know the certainty of the words of truth" (Prov 22:21).

Theology debates whether our future is predetermined or decided by our free will.

The Bible says, "but now [God] commandeth all men every where to repent" (Acts 17:30).

Theology argues whether men who have never heard the gospel can be saved.

The Bible says, "It pleased God by the foolishness of preaching to save them that believe," and "how shall they hear without a preacher?" (1 Cor 1:21, Rom 10:14).

Theology does not preach.

The Bible must be preached to be believed (Rom 10:17).

_____

Theology is more palatable to unbelievers and skeptics.

The Bible will not work effectually in those who do not believe (1 Thess 2:13).

_____

Theology can often change.

The Bible never changes (Isa 40:8).

_____

Theology is man's word about God.

The Bible is God's word to man (2 Tim 3:16).

_____

The mind of a wise man is required to study theology.

The mind of God is required to study the Bible (1 Cor 2:12-16).

Part II

UNDERSTANDING RIGHT DIVISION

"Study to shew thyself approved unto God, a workman that needeth not to be ashamed, rightly dividing the word of truth."
- 2 Timothy 2:15

CHAPTER 4

APPROACHING SCRIPTURE

Eating lobster is an exercise of faith. You order it believing you will get succulent, meaty seafood, but what you see is a shell-covered crustacean and a mallet to make sure it is dead. Where's the meat? It's in there, but it takes some work to find. If you try to bite into it immediately, you can break your teeth.

The same result occurs if you try to dig into your Bible without first rightly dividing. You want to enjoy the pleasures of God's word but end up choking on passages that are not about us.

"But there is so much in the Bible that is not about me. Where is my meat?"

And so it is with lobster: when you are done with the meal, there are more inedible bits on the plate than meat that you ate. But the meat is very good. You cannot enjoy lobster unless you know to crack it open and find the meat. And so it is with the Bible.

WHY YOU THINK THE BIBLE IS HARD TO UNDERSTAND

The reason most people think the Bible is too hard to understand is that they do not rightly divide the word of truth. This means they think that every verse in the Bible is written for their obedience and personal application.

God revealed his law in the Bible. Yet one place tells us that we are subject to it, while another tells us those who desire to teach it now are vain (Deu 32:47 and 1 Tim 1:6-7).

In one verse circumcision is a matter of salvation, while on another page it voids the cross of Christ (Gen 17:14; Gal 5:2)!

What about the Sabbath day? In one section it is a commandment. In another, the Lord of the Sabbath supersedes it. Yet in another, we are not to let anyone judge us about it (Exo 20:10; Mat 12:2-8; Col 2:16).

Is our justification based on our works or not? (Rom 4:5; James 2:24)

It is no wonder the Bible can be confusing. Confusion is compounded when preachers do not rightly divide. It is easy to see through pastors and teachers making excuses, avoiding, or distorting the passages in attempt to reconcile them. If only they knew how to rightly divide, all of these confusions would become clear.

In all these examples, it could be said the confusion is created by what Paul wrote in his epistles. There is a reason for that: the Lord Jesus Christ gave a special revelation to the Apostle Paul. This revelation contained a previously unknown message of hope and salvation among the Gentiles and explains why what Paul teaches is so different from what is found elsewhere in scripture (Col 1:25-27).

This dispensation of the Lord given to Paul is called a mystery and is distinct from the information found in the law and the prophets (Eph 3:3-5). When we separate or draw a line of division between God's information in prophecy and his mystery information now revealed to Paul, we begin to see how the entire Bible fits in God's eternal purpose.

The instructions for the church today are found in Paul's doctrine, the preaching of Jesus Christ according to the revelation of the mystery (2 Tim 2:7). Without rightly dividing prophecy from mystery, the Bible can be hard to understand.

THREE KINDS OF BIBLE APPLICATION

It is necessary in Bible lessons to have an application. Without it, the lesson has no practical benefit. There are three kinds of Bible application. Ignoring any of them can lead to misunderstanding.

#1: HISTORICAL APPLICATION

The Bible is accurate in all of its descriptions of people, places, events, and words. It is truly inspired by God. Any question of the Bible's inerrancy must be answered using a form of historical application. Apologists and students of prophecy place their application emphasis here, but any application of the Bible must believe the Bible to be factual or it will not be based in reality.

Bible belief, as a true record of God's inspired words, engenders faith. Without this historical truth, the Bible becomes an imaginative man-made storybook filled with anachronisms.

Overemphasizing the historical application can lead to a scientific approach to the Bible that appears cold and distant. The historical application is important in our study of every passage of the Bible but must be accompanied by spiritual and dispensational applications.

#2: SPIRITUAL APPLICATION

In the Bible alone we learn about God, his character, holiness, and anything that has virtue. The spiritual application allows us to grow in godliness. Any question of what is good must be answered using a form of spiritual application. Many devotionals and moral literature use this application to communicate good manners.

This application teaches us what it is like to walk in the Spirit. Without this spiritual instruction, believers revert to the works of the flesh and live a carnal life without a zeal for good works. The Bible becomes a book of general morality and is not meaningful.

Overemphasizing the spiritual application can lead to a bland or false spirituality that ignores doctrine and compromises the truth for the sake of unity. A spiritual application is useful for learning from all scripture but must be balanced by the historical and doctrinal applications.

#3: DOCTRINAL APPLICATION

The Bible is where we discover the instructions for our direct involvement in God's will. This type of doctrinal application is always subject to the context, which is why this application is sometimes called the dispensational application. This application asks, what is God telling me to do? What is God's will in this passage? Am I in the intended audience?

Active participation in any instruction from God must first consider the doctrinal application. Doctrinal applications are not popular since they require more study to know who is speaking and to whom and require avoiding doctrines that are not instructions to us. All scripture is profitable for doctrine, but not all doctrine is for our participation.

Without the doctrinal application the believer is confused about what God is telling him to do. Activities such as prayer, Bible study, holy days, and salvation become confusing. Right division encourages the doctrinal understanding of all of scripture and helps to eliminate the confusion.

It is hard to overemphasize this application since it is mostly absent from most Biblical application. When the doctrinal application ignores the historical or spiritual applications then it can produce heresies, pride, and bad manners.

Ignoring any of these three Bible applications can make the Bible unprofitable. All scripture is profitable, and using all three kinds of Biblical application makes it so.

CHAPTER 5
FINDING INSTRUCTIONS

A traffic light gives contradicting instructions at the same time: one light is red, while another light is green. Both messages are right; neither is a mistake, because they are directed at cars on different roads.

We must know which instruction is given to us. Are we to stop, or are we to go? These contradicting instructions are given to certain people at certain places for certain times. We cannot just pick which color we want to obey. If the red light people were to follow the green light's instructions, there would be chaos, things would be confusing, and people would get hurt.

This same effect happens when we do not apply discernment in whether differing instructions in the Bible are written to us or to other people going a different direction.

IS ALL THE BIBLE WRITTEN FOR US?

Contradictory instructions force us to choose to obey one or the other. This is where rightly dividing the word of truth becomes profitable.

Rightly dividing the word of truth does not remove any Scripture from our profit. God forbid we eliminate or ignore one word, syllable, or punctuation from the complete sacred text of God's perfect word!

Instead, right division is like dividing a book into its index or a speech into its outline. By separating the parts into their appropriate context, we are in a better position to understand the whole.

The entire Bible is written for us, but not every verse is addressed to us or written about us. All scripture is profitable, but not every passage is for our participation or obedience.

THE IMPORTANCE OF "ALL SCRIPTURE"

A popular attack on dispensational Bible study is to claim that it eliminates most of the Bible as applicable to us. Even many young dispensationalists develop a false fear of reading or applying truth from Old Testament passages. However, this is a misunderstanding of what it means to rightly divide the word of truth.

In no sense would students of the Bible be better off by ignoring certain books or rejecting books as beneficial for our profit and application.

"All scripture is given by inspiration of God, and is profitable for doctrine, for reproof, for correction, for instruction in righteousness..."   −2 Timothy 3:16

By right division, I mean acknowledging that the doctrine concerning the church today is found in Paul's epistles alone by the revelation of Jesus Christ. This dispensation given to Paul was hidden in ages past, kept secret since the world began (Rom 16:25; Col 1:25-26; 2 Tim 2:7-15). That this mystery information was kept secret since the world began does not diminish the benefit that can be gained from the rest of the Bible.

How would we know sin if it were not by the law? (Rom 3:19; Rom 7:7; 1 John 3:4)

How would we know of imputed righteousness if we could not read what "Abraham our Father, pertaining to the flesh, hath found?" (Romans 4:1-3)

How would we fear examples of God's hatred toward unrighteousness unless we read about how Israel lusted after evil things in the wilderness and was overthrown? (1 Corinthians 10:6)

It is from our own apostle that we read that all scripture is profitable for our learning.

"For whatsoever things were written aforetime were written for our learning, that we through patience and comfort of the scriptures might have hope."

– Romans 15:4

These same scriptures give witness to the death and resurrection of Jesus Christ, which is essential to the gospel that we preach today (1 Corinthians 15:1-4)! It should be evident that every word in the Bible is written for our edification and profit.

RIGHT DIVISION

Right division allows us to understand difficult passages by acknowledging the intended audience may not be the church today. While every book and testament is written for us to learn from, not every book and testament is written to us for participation.

Surely we can agree that when God told Noah to build an ark, he was speaking to Noah and not to anyone in the mystery church revealed first to Paul. Once realizing the proper context and audience, we can understand the limits of its application. While we could learn the spiritual truths about Noah's example of righteous obedience or his faithful diligence in an evil world, we would be wrong to follow Noah and build an ark simply because it is in the Bible and "since God said it, I'm supposed to obey it."

This extreme example is intended to show the error of taking any verse of Scripture as instruction for us without first rightly dividing. We would be wise to interpret every passage in its dispensational context before applying its instruction to us.

Choosing not to rightly divide a passage into its dispensational context is the cause of much biblical confusion, error, and misinterpretation in the church. God did not write all scripture to us. Rightly dividing God's changing instructions to whom he gave them can cure the confusion.

CONSISTENT INTERPRETATION

Without right division, contradictions abound that force sincere Christians to pick some verses and ignore others, but how do they pick? If they do not rightly divide the mystery given to Paul from the purpose God has for Israel, on what basis do they choose?

Attempting to obey every instruction in the Bible outside of its dispensational context will produce contradictions. Often times, when Christians are asked why they pick one verse and not the other, they ignorantly proclaim that every verse in the Bible should be obeyed equally. It is impossible to obey every command in the Bible at the same time. Therefore, what they say and what they do are very different.

As an example, concerning our zealous missionary efforts, do we go to Gentile nations to preach the gospel? Jesus told the disciples in Matthew 10:5 to "Go not into the way of the Gentiles," but in Acts 22:21 the same Jesus tells Paul to go to the Gentiles:

"Depart: for I will send thee far hence unto the Gentiles."
– Acts 22:21

We cannot obey both instructions at the same time. The solution should be obvious: what Jesus told the disciples was not given to the apostle Paul to obey in his ministry. The question the church should be asking is whether we follow the Lord's instructions to the twelve disciples or the Lord's instructions to the apostle Paul. The answer is found in rightly dividing the word of truth.

If all scripture is going to be profitable, then it must be rightly divided. Not all scripture is written to us. If we pretend it is, then the scripture becomes unprofitable, contradictory, and the cause of hypocrisy.

Rightly dividing the word of truth allows us to see with clarity God's eternal purpose on every page as well as his specific instructions to us found in Paul's epistles.

CHOOSING YOUR PART OF THE BIBLE

Though we might have a heart of submission to do anything the Lord instructs, it is impossible to do everything the Bible teaches. The Bible contains God's instructions to various people over the course of thousands of years. It is impossible to do everything the Bible says to do. No one ever has, because no one can.

Everyone must discern which part of the Bible is for their participation and then choose to obey *that*. Everyone must choose. Those who claim not to pick and choose are simply ignoring the differing instructions in the 66-book, inspired Bible. Which doctrinal camp you belong to will depend upon *how* you choose.

Mainline Christians may choose the red letters because they were the words of Jesus. Yet, was not all of scripture inspired by God (2 Tim 3:16)? Most of our chief doctrines are found in the black letters.

Pentecostals try to "do more" of the Bible and choose Acts 2 as their place of instruction. After all, the disciples had a ministry after Jesus' resurrection that began at Pentecost.

Dominionists desire to "take back America," and so they choose to use the dominion language of the law given to God's only nation: Israel.

Tithe-teachers who need some extra money in a recession choose to teach Old Testament curse passages to milk their members.

When churches try to "seek a vision" from God, they will strip a seemingly random verse from the Bible out of its context and use it as a driving force for some social action campaign. Why did they choose that verse? Instead of an objective reason, the answer is typically something mystical, subjective, and secretive such as, "the Lord led me," or "it was laid upon my heart."

How to Choose

How do we choose rightly and objectively? Instead of flipping the doctrinal coin, here is a better way:

After reading a passage of the Bible, ask, "Who is speaking?" There are times in the Bible that Satan's lies are recorded. Avoid participating in his lies. Secondly, ask, "To whom are they speaking? Do I fit in the audience?" God gave instructions to Isaiah to preach without clothes (Isa 20:2). You are not Isaiah, a prophet to Israel. Leave those instructions alone.

Finally, ask, "Are there any later instructions from the Lord that replace this instruction?" You will be amazed at the problems this resolves. Everyone divides or chooses which parts of the Bible they will obey. This method will help you to rightly divide.

The Best Choice

Asking these questions of Bible passages will lead you to one place: Paul's epistles. Jesus appeared to Paul and taught him the manifold wisdom of God (Gal 1:1 & 11; Eph 3:10). His epistles contain instructions from the Lord Jesus. While most of your Bible was written specifically to the nation of Israel, the Lord gave Paul instructions specifically for the Gentiles (Eph 3:1). He was titled the "apostle of the Gentiles" (Rom 11:13). You are in this audience.

The Lord Jesus revealed the mystery of himself to Paul after the red letters and after Pentecost. Paul claims to be the last person to see the resurrected Lord (1 Cor 15:8). He was given the preaching of the cross and the gospel of the grace of God as a pattern for our present salvation (1 Tim 1:15-16). There has been no further revelation that has superseded the instructions God inspired in the Pauline epistles.

Everyone chooses which part of the Bible to obey. Contextual guidelines lead you to only one conclusion. Choose the only place you will find the teaching of Jesus Christ to Gentiles according to the revelation of the mystery (Rom 16:25). In Paul's epistles alone the doctrines exist that work today for the church, the Body of Christ.

HOW TO RIGHTLY DIVIDE

I remember once talking to a man zealous for God who told me that he obeyed "everything in the Bible!" His heart to obey anything the Lord instructed was admirable. Yet, it is impossible to obey every instruction from the Lord in the Bible! There are instructions from the Lord that conflict with earlier instructions, instructions that are no longer feasible, or instructions not for our obedience. We would never think of following God's instructions to Noah to build an ark or his instruction for Peter to walk on water. We must understand the context of the instructions and obey those that God intends the church to obey.

Our job then is to discern which instructions we should obey and which we should not, the reasons why, and the context in which they should be obeyed. This is what we call dispensational Bible study, or right division.

QUESTION THE CONTEXT

Everyone divides the Bible in some way, and no one thinks they wrongly divide. To determine the context of a passage, merely ask the interrogative questions: who, what, when, where, why? Here are some simple questions to ask to determine the context of a passage:

1) Who is speaking and to whom?
2) What are they speaking about?
3) When are they speaking about it?
4) Why are they speaking about it?

The answers to these questions will establish a context for the passage. Sometimes you will not be able to answer all the questions. If not, answer what you can. Not all the answers are necessary for understanding.

ARE YOU IN THE CONTEXT?

Next, you must determine if you fit in the context of the passage. If you do, then obey; if not, then you must let it be as instructions not written to you. For example, if the Devil is speaking, you can determine that the lying words that come out of his mouth are not for you to obey. If God is telling Noah to build an ark, you can determine that you are not in that audience since the Flood is already past.

If God is speaking about making a covenant with Israel, you can also determine that you are not in the context since you are not Israel (if you are a Jew reading this then there are other questions you must ask).

Rightly dividing God's dispensations

If we ask these questions throughout the scriptures, we find that many passages have the same context. We call these specific doctrinal contexts describing God's relation to man "dispensations."

We are living in the dispensation of God's grace where Jesus gave instructions to the apostle Paul that are more excellent for us than the instructions in other dispensations (Phil 1:10; Eph 3:2). The Lord's instructions to Paul revealed a mystery not known before in other ages (Col 1:26; Eph 3:5). This constituted a new context or dispensation that changed the relationship between God and man. This dispensation of God's instructions was the last given and must be rightly divided from the others (1 Cor 15:8).

A failure to rightly divide the mystery information given to Paul (Rom 16:25) from the prophecy information given to God's prophets since the world began (Acts 3:21) produces significant doctrinal confusion (2 Tim 2:7). But don't take my word for it.

"Study to shew thyself approved unto God, a workman that needeth not to be ashamed, rightly dividing the word of truth."

– 2 Timothy 2:15

CHAPTER 6

THE IMPORTANCE OF
RIGHT DIVISION

The earliest English concordances were published in the 16th century. Since then, they have become an invaluable tool in Bible study. Computers' searching capabilities have made long hours of collecting words from the Bible a task that takes only a few seconds. Yet, concordances and word search software fail at the point of context. It is not enough to find every instance of a word in the Bible. Every word must be rightly divided; it must be put in its proper dispensational context.

CONTEXT AND DEFINITION

The context can greatly affect definition. It is proper to say, "My salary went *down*," which means that the amount of money decreased. It is also possible to say, "I went *down* to Mexico," which means I traveled south. It is the same with important words in your Bible such as faith, belief, salvation, grace, and gospel. Noah found grace in the eyes of the Lord (Gen 6:8). Yet, this must be different than the grace which is pictured by the cross work of Christ (Eph 2:5).

Abraham's belief in the Lord was counted for righteousness in Genesis 15:6. Yet Abraham did not know the gospel of salvation through the blood of Christ in Ephesians 1:13 that we are called to believe upon today.

In the same monologue, Zacharias uses salvation to describe both salvation from political enemies and salvation from sins (Luke 1:69 and 77).

Romans 1:17 quotes Habakkuk 2:4 when it states the truth that "the just shall live by faith." However, faith in the Messiah was not possible until he arrived centuries after the law was given. Faith in Jesus' work on the cross was not revealed until Paul was given apostleship.

Faith must be identified dispensationally to understand the content of faith. A concordance fails to provide the dispensational context.

THE NEED FOR RIGHT DIVISION

Ignoring the rightly divided context has introduced serious errors into the church's presentation of the gospel. The same word "gospel" is used many times in the Bible, but it is not the same message every time. The gospel taught by the disciples and Jesus in Luke 9:6 is not the same gospel that Jesus told Paul to teach. The gospel in Luke 9:6 did not include the meaning of the cross, because they did not understand it (Luke 18:32-34)! Paul's gospel was the preaching of the cross for salvation (1 Cor 1:18, 15:1-4).

While it is necessary and useful to compile a list of every word instance in the Bible as in concordances, the work is not yet done. To be the workman that will not be ashamed, we must rightly divide the word of truth (2 Tim 2:15).

HOW TO FIND GEMS IN YOUR BIBLE STUDY

Bible study is often described as digging for gems and jewels. For knowledgeable diggers, the Bible is a rich mine.

"I rejoice at thy word, as one that findeth great spoil."
– Psalm 119:162

Studying the Bible can reap significant riches, but for many people the Bible is an impenetrable book. Their shovels cannot break ground, and when they do it seems only to be a dirty mess without any real profit. They pursue endless book summaries, gospel harmonies, psalm devotionals, and character studies and always seem to come up short of anything substantial about God's will and purpose.

The more technical student dives into grammar studies, figures of speech, chronologies, ancient culture, and maps. Yet, for so much effort, only a few shiny stones are uncovered. Like the story of Ali Hafed in "Acres of Diamonds,[1]" they cannot seem to locate where the diamonds are or how to find them, and then end up quitting Bible study in despair. Yet, the diamonds are there! The riches are in God's word. I have seen them. They may be right under your nose!

---

[1] Conwell, Russel H., and John Wannamaker. *Acres of Diamonds.* Executive Books, 2004. Print.

USING THE PROPER TOOLS

If digging into Bible study feels like tilling a garden with a kitchen knife, then perhaps you need to get a better tool. Use this tool of right division to sift out gems in your Bible study: separate prophecy from mystery. Identify the passages referring to God's prophetic purpose with Israel, and separate them in your mind from the passages talking about God's mystery purpose to the Body of Christ.

Peter describes the purpose of God for Israel as being "spoken by the mouth of all his holy prophets since the world began" (Acts 3:21). Paul describes the purpose of God for the Body of Christ as being "kept secret since the world began" (Rom 16:25).

The prophetic purpose will be fulfilled in the earth. It started in Genesis 1 and will end in Revelation. The mystery purpose completes God's will in heavenly places. Paul's epistles alone reveal the mystery and describe the time in which you now live. Paul says it is his duty to "preach among the Gentiles the unsearchable riches of Christ; and to make all men see what is the fellowship of the mystery" (Eph 3:8-9). It is in God's epistles through Paul, separated from the ministry of Peter and Jesus' ministry to Israel, that we will find large jewels well prepared for our use.

ACRES OF DIAMONDS

When they are rightly divided even the prophetic passages of the Old Testament, the psalms, synoptics, and Hebrew epistles (none of which describe our dispensation) start to reveal jewels for us to gaze upon.

At one time these passages were murky and clear as mud. When rightly divided from mystery, they are now clear and sparkly jewels in their own right. Although they are not jewels we can call our own, they are great spoils to God's chosen people that will be realized in the future (Rom 11:33).

Stop trying to harmonize the red letters and spiritualize Jesus' teachings to Israel since they were never for your participation. Set aside the character studies of Peter, David, and the twelve apostles and learn the mystery of Christ that none of them knew.

When we do not use the tool of right division to separate prophecy from mystery, then our digging into the word of God will be difficult and strenuous.

"To whom God would make known what is the riches of the glory of this mystery among the Gentiles"
– Colossians 1:27

Using the right tool the right way reveals the scriptures to be acres of diamonds where there was once just a bunch of dirt.

"...unto all riches of the full assurance of understanding, to the acknowledgement of the mystery of God, and of the Father, and of Christ; In whom are hid all the treasures of wisdom and knowledge."
– Colossians 2:2-3

9 HARBINGERS OF BAD DOCTRINE

Taking the Bible literally creates teachers of prophecy. Taking the Bible literally but failing to rightly divide prophecy from mystery creates bad doctrine.

For millennia, Bible literalists who failed to rightly divide have taught that prophetic fulfillment in the current events of their time. Self-proclaimed prophecy gurus are ignorant of the present dispensation of God's grace wherein God is reconciled to the world not imputing trespasses. They continue to teach that these are the "last days" just as Peter taught 2000 years ago at Pentecost and that current events are signs of God's impending judgment, just as the Bible predicted for Israel.

The latest prophetic innovation is the nine harbingers of God's judgment on America discovered by best-selling author, Jonathan Cahn, in his DVD and books about the Isaiah 9:10 judgment[2].

Harbingers are warnings or signs. Patterned after Rabbi Cahn, here are nine harbingers that will help you identify a teacher of prophecy that understands neither how to rightly divide nor what God is doing today:

1st Harbinger: Using Israel as Your Pattern

Israel was a nation uniquely chosen by God to possess his promises for earthly dominion. God has not dealt like he did with Israel with any other nation (Psa 147:20). No other nation past or present has God's covenanted "hedge of protection."

---

[2] Originally, there was a movie with Jonathan Cahn explaining the Isaiah 9:10 judgment and the nine harbingers of judgment on America. His book *The Harbinger* went on to be a bestseller in 2012.

When a teacher claims that how God worked with Israel is the pattern for you or your country, turn around and walk away.

2nd Harbinger: Genealogies

When the application of current events to Bible prophecies depends on genealogies, turn off the radio. Genealogies minister questions and entangle divine prophecies with races. These racial prophecies have been fodder for loads of bad doctrine and a few wars[3].

> "Neither give heed to fables and endless genealogies, which minister questions, rather than godly edifying which is in faith: so do."   – 1 Timothy 1:4

Just because Assyrians were Israel's enemies in Isaiah 9 does not mean they are divinely ordained to be ours in the 21st century.

3rd Harbinger: Crisis Centered

Every generation has a crisis. When prophetic teachers say that God is speaking through the national or global crisis of your generation, take a deep breath and remember 2 Corinthians 12:10.

---

[3] Gen 9:25-27 was taught wrongly in America during the 18-19th centuries to justify slavery and racism. Shamefully, Bible teachers in the 20-21st centuries (Feldick, Jordan, Morris, Custance, etc.) continue the misinterpretation of Genesis 9 by teaching divine destiny and responsibility for different races. The cure for this type of wrong doctrine is right division which not only places Noah's sons in a different dispensational context, but recognizes according to the mystery there is no gender, nationality, economic status, or race in Christ in heaven or on earth (Gal 3:28).

The bubonic plague was said to be a fulfillment of Revelation, as was Pearl Harbor, JFK's assassination, 9/11, and the Great Recession of 2008. Many people have died, and many bricks have fallen throughout history.

Why is the current generation always more unique than the rest? We are closer to the end than we have ever been before, but both Paul and the Lord tell us not to be troubled when we see present crises (Matt 24:6; 2 Thess 2:2-3).

4th Harbinger: Adding to Scripture

When a teacher of prophecy has to add to scripture to make his prophecy work, then it is time to change the channel. Isaiah 9:10 never mentions Israel's intent to build their towers taller, yet that is what rabbi Cahn adds and makes his 4th harbinger. Israel's defiance of God to use hewn stones instead of unhewn stones was always contrary to the law of God. That towers are built in New York City in the 21st century out of hewn stones means nothing when the Bible is rightly divided. The church can build a pyramid out of hewn stones, and it would not be violating God's instructions for today.

5th Harbinger: Spiritualizing

It might seem strange that a Bible-literalist prophecy teacher would be guilty of spiritualizing the Bible, but that is what must happen to force Israel's prophecies into fulfillment in 21st century America. If we take them literally, they are simply not happening as the Bible says they would. Beware of those who say prophecy is being literally fulfilled, but only if the definition of literally means "figuratively," "similarly," or "in parallel," and not the plain meaning of the text. If the Bible does not identify the figure, then the teacher is a spiritual spin-doctor and should be literally avoided like a metaphorical plague.

6th Harbinger: Taking Away from Scripture

If a word does not fit the prophecy, just take it out. According to Rabbi Cahn's sixth harbinger, the sycamore tree is literal, but the phrase "cut down" in Isaiah 9:10 is just a metaphor for "knocked down by a falling building" on September 11, 2001. Metaphors exist in the Bible, but they must be correctly identified and consistently interpreted. Otherwise, important details are removed from scripture, a practice we should be careful to avoid (Rev 22:19).

7th Harbinger: Excessive Use of Hebrew or Greek

Nothing dazzles the mind like a speaker of tongues, and by tongues I mean languages. It is commonplace for prophetic teachers to enlighten you about the hidden meaning made by linguistic leaps of faith. Beware! These can jump you right off the cliff of context.

8th Harbinger: Inventing New Covenants

The promises and the covenants God gave in the Bible are sufficient for his will. When a teacher tries to play "Let's make a deal" and binds you to a new curse or blessing from God, avoid such a one. You have met someone who is liable to beguile you of your reward (Colossians 2:18).

9th Harbinger: Problems Counting

Numbers and dates are important to the teacher of prophecy. However, math is not always his strong suit. Prophetic numbers not lining up can be disastrous for teachers like Hal Lindsey in "Late Great Planet Earth" or Harold Camping in 1994 (and 2011).

God wants you to give 310 dollars because of Malachi 3:10? There are nine signs from Isaiah 9:10? Luke 20:13 says the Lord will return in 2013? No, that is not real Bible study; that is numerological superstition.

When the main support for a teaching is mind-boggling or coincidental calculations do not wait around for things not to work out. Leave early.

CONCLUSION

The Bible should be taken literally, but a failure to rightly divide prophecy from mystery in the Bible creates all sorts of bad doctrine and false applications from prophecy to today.

It is well known that Bible prophecy teachers rise in popularity when society is in decline. Bad prophecy teachers give divine explanations to simple-minded people, ignore the real cause of the world's problems, and obscure what God is doing today through the church. If we stop blaming God for current events, then we might be able to start serving the Lord despite them.

Remember these nine harbingers, and do the work of an ambassador of God's grace speaking the things which become sound doctrine (Titus 2:1).

It Takes Work

It takes work to rightly divide the Bible.

First, read and learn all of God's revelations in the Bible. Rightly dividing the word of truth is impossible if you have not first found what needs divided.

Second, discern what and what manner of time God was speaking. This is called dispensational Bible study.

Third, rightly divide the differences created by God's dispensations. If you cannot find any differences, go back to step one.

Salvation is not of works, but we grow spiritually according to the work we put in to studying and applying the Bible rightly divided. Rightly dividing the Bible takes work. We were made to be workmen (Eph 2:10).

"Study to shew thyself approved unto God, a workman that needeth not to be ashamed, rightly dividing the word of truth."   – 2 Timothy 2:15

Part III

DISTINGUISHING DISPENSATIONS

"If ye have heard of the dispensation of the grace of God which is given me to you-ward: how that by revelation he made known unto me the mystery…"
- Ephesians 3:2-3

CHAPTER 7

DISPENSATIONS IN THE BIBLE

Studying the Bible dispensationally is not an invented theology. It is consistently the natural product of believing the Bible and taking it literally, and men who do so come independently to the same conclusion[1]. While people will debate over what is a dispensation and their number, no one can dispute that the word itself is in the Bible and must be interpreted.

Paul was given a dispensation (Eph 3:2). There were different revelations from God at sundry times (Heb 1:1). Some of these revelations dispense new information about how he deals with us and how we ought to respond in faith. Places like Ephesians 2, Galatians 3, and Romans 5 explain changes that occur because of God's revelations and dispensations.

---

[1] While Darby is credited with originating dispensationalism, covenant theologians like Jonathan Edwards and Isaac Watts identified dispensations long before Darby as a means of explaining God's progressive revelation. Darby's unique contribution concerned the separation of the mystery church from prophecy.

Starting from scratch, a person can easily distinguish dispensations. The scratch ingredients are:

(1) A God that is true
(2) A Bible that is without error
(3) A person willing to read it literally

You do not need a dispensational systematic theology to teach you the fundamentals of dispensational Bible study; you need a Bible you can believe.

GOD'S TWO-FOLD PLAN AND PURPOSE

An important discovery of dispensational Bible study is the doctrine of God's two-fold plan revealed in Scripture. Rightly dividing the word of truth at this fold line allows us to see clearly how God's ultimate purpose for both folds comes together in Christ.

Where is this right division? While it is popular to think this most important division is between the Old and New Testaments, that would be wrong. The most essential distinction we can make is the difference between prophecy and mystery.

PROPHECY – GOD'S PLAN FOR THE EARTH

The subject of prophecy pertains to God's revealed plan to reign and rule over the earth. This part of God's plan uses the nation Israel as the channel of blessing to the entire world (Gen 12:2-3; Isa 2:2). The information in prophecy culminates in the Lord's coming to earth where he will set up his kingdom in Zion for ever (Micah 4:7). Zacharias sums up this body of information as consisting of what was spoken by the prophets since the world began:

> "As he spake by the mouth of his holy prophets, which have been since the world began"   – Luke 1:70

Peter also taught this same prophetic plan made known from the foundation of the world:

> "… which God hath spoken by the mouth of all his holy prophets since the world began."   – Acts 3:21

MYSTERY – GOD'S PLAN FOR THE HEAVENS

The subject of the revelation of the mystery pertains to God's plan to reign and rule in heaven (Phi 3:20; Eph 2:6). This part of God's plan uses a new creature, without national distinction or status (2 Cor 5:17; Gal 3:28). This corporate body resides under the authority of Christ as the head and is known as the Body of Christ, or simply, the Church (Eph 4:12; 1 Cor 12:27). The mystery information culminates in the Lord's receiving of the saints to reign and rule in heavenly places forever (1 Thess 4:16-17).

This information is distinguished by the clear statements made by Paul that it was not part of prophecy:

> "…according to my gospel, and the preaching of Jesus Christ, according to the revelation of the mystery, which was kept secret since the world began," – Romans 16:25
> "And to make all men see what is the fellowship of the

mystery, which from the beginning of the world hath been hid in God, who created all things by Jesus Christ:"

– Ephesians 3:9

RIGHTLY DIVIDING THE WORD OF TRUTH

Understanding this primary distinction in God's two-fold plan, one for the earth revealed in prophecy and the other for heavenly places in the revelation of the mystery, is the key to rightly dividing the word of truth (2 Tim 2:15). It is right to divide those instructions pertaining to prophecy from the specific information revealed in the mystery. Well-informed soldiers are better equipped for battle, and well-informed saints are better equipped to please him who died for them if we know which instructions we are to obey (2 Tim 2:4).

As we recognize the two-fold plan of God we can also better recognize God's ultimate purpose for all things, both in heaven and earth, to be in Christ.

"That in the dispensation of the fulness of times he might gather together in one all things in Christ, both which are in heaven, and which are on earth; even in him:"

– Ephesians 1:10

Whereas, "in the beginning God created the heaven and the earth," the Bible rightly divided reveals God's two-fold plan to ultimately reign and rule over both the heaven and the earth in Christ.

SOME NECESSARY DIVISIONS

There are three divisions that, when recognized, will give a tremendous boost in understanding the Bible. When their differences are not fully appreciated, confusion arises. Most of church history has been plagued with Bible difficulties by wrongfully ignoring these necessary divisions:

1. LAW / GRACE

Law and grace are the two principles by which mankind has operated with God. The first law was given to Adam and Eve. Later, hundreds were given in covenant with Israel. We learn from the law the need for a great work to be done for God's righteousness.

Grace is epitomized in the great dispensation of grace in which we now live. It describes undeserved favor toward reprobate humanity. God's provision of free grace is offered to all without works. God's love is manifested in the finished work of Christ on the cross.

While both principles magnify the Lord Jesus Christ, they must be separated if we are to avoid doctrinal confusion. We are either under law or under grace.

2. ISRAEL / CHURCH

Israel and the Church are the two entities through which God's will is performed. Israel gives purpose to religion, being the only religion ever ordained by God. Through its covenants, this one great nation of priests shadowed the greater things to come on earth through the Messiah.

The Church, in this case, is not the general congregation throughout all history, but that unique, one-body church which is called the body of Christ. In every aspect, this new creature represents the power of God's grace through faith. Through faith the gospel of Christ creates all things new, manifesting God's glory in heavenly places.

While both entities point to the Lord Jesus Christ for their fulfillment, they must be separated if we are to avoid identity confusion. God's people in the Bible are either identified by Israel (more aptly Jew or Gentile), or they are identified by the Church the body of Christ (neither Jew nor Gentile).

3. EARTH / HEAVEN

Heaven and earth are the two spheres of dominion that God has purposed to glorify him, but since the beginning they have been usurped by Satan through sin. In the end, the home of lowly mankind, earth, will become the centerpiece of God's kingdom. Israel will declare the marvelous works of God manifest in the flesh who keeps promises through all ages.

Heavenly places have always been the realm of angels and other spiritual beings. In the end, heaven will be filled with grace-gifted members of the new creature. The one body will declare the riches of his grace through Christ in the very places where the great rebellion started in the universe.

While both dominions will eventually be gathered together in Christ, they must now be separated if we are to avoid ministry confusion. Israel will minister as citizens of an earthly kingdom through the covenants. The church is now currently ministering as ambassadors building a body fit for heavenly places (2 Cor 5:20-21; Eph 2:6-7).

PROPHECY / MYSTERY

The three necessary divisions can be simplified into the general division between prophecy and mystery. The law, Israel, and the earth are the subjects of prophecy, which had been spoken since the world began until Paul (Acts 3:18-24).

Grace, the one body Church, and heavenly places are the subjects of the mystery of Christ, which had been kept secret until revealed to the apostle Paul (Rom 16:25). We now live in this dispensation.

A failure to rightly divide these pairs has turned the Bible into a conglomeration of confusion. Do not try to put together what God has separated. Making these distinctions clear will greatly benefit anyone who desires to grow in their understanding of God and the Bible.

DISPENSATIONAL CHANGES

When God reveals information that changes the prophetic context, then we need to place a division in the scripture. The new information divides from the old information. This creates contexts by which we can interpret all of scripture. This is what we call dispensational change. Paul calls the information he received from the Lord a dispensation (Col 1:25). This information changed the prophetic context of God's instructions. According to Paul's teaching, God is dealing with different people, through a different apostle, in a different way, by a different gospel, towards a different destination. That is a lot of change.

A smaller change occurred between Abraham and Moses. Abraham was given the promises of God and the covenant of circumcision (Gen 17:1-10). Four hundred years later, the law was added because of transgressions (Gal 3:17). The law did not remove the promises, but rather, made them a part of a testament. Abraham was not under the Old Testament known as the Mosaic covenant.

Another change occurred when Jesus' earthly ministry prepared the way for the New Testament. The New Testament could not be in effect until after Christ died (Heb 9:16-17). Jesus was born under the Old Testament and died to institute the New Testament (Gal 4:4). The New Testament replaced the Old, but it could not remove the promises and was given to the same people who received the Old Testament (Heb 8:10). The covenant of circumcision and promises to the fathers were being fulfilled by a change in the law and the priesthood (Heb 7:12).

When the kingdom comes, there will be another dispensational change as the promises are kept by God and the kingdom of heaven comes to earth beginning at Jerusalem (Luke 24:47). This is made possible by the full operation of the New Testament promises.

All of these changes were prophesied and revealed in God's purpose to Israel. We can read about them in the prophets and the Hebrew epistles. The dispensational change given to Paul was separate from prophecy entirely. It is written that the mystery revealed to Paul "was kept secret since the world began" (Rom 16:25).

When reading Paul's epistles we are reading about a change more excellent than the changes between Abraham and Moses, the Old Testament and New Testament, or even the kingdom come. We are reading about the revelation of the mystery of God in Christ to pay for the sins of humanity without a covenant or a law system (Rom 3:22): no priests, no sacrifices, no covenants, no holy days, no Israel, no land promise. In the mystery of Christ, God revealed information that changed the prophetic context of the time in which we live. We now no longer live in a time that was prophesied since the world began. We now live in a dispensation that is called a Mystery.

IT IS RIGHT TO DIVIDE WHAT IS DIFFERENT

Similarities in the Bible are found before differences. It is easy to find similarities. Doing a simple concordance search can reveal many similar words, verses, and themes. However, study that is more careful is required to identify the differences. Rightly dividing the Bible requires recognizing the differences in God's instructions. Those who cannot see the dividing lines in your Bible will think God's instructions are the same for everyone on every page.

Different baptisms become the same baptism. Different gospels become the same gospel. Some even go so far as to call the entire Bible "the gospel" as if all parts are equally sufficient to save someone. This type of overgeneralization may feel spiritual, but it hinders dispensational Bible study that requires a more careful analysis of God's instructions.

A SIMPLE DIFFERENCE

One difference is sufficient to show that not all is the same. There are hundreds of differences in God's instructions in your Bible. (Differences are not mistakes.)

Genesis 17 required all God's people be circumcised, or else be cut off from God's covenant (Gen 17:14). Galatians 5:6 says that circumcision does not avail anything. So, which is it? You cannot teach both at the same time.

Leviticus 11:2 restricts the meat that could be eaten by law-abiding Jews. However, Paul says in 1 Timothy 4:2 that nothing is to be refused and even calls abstaining from meats a doctrine of devils! This is quite a difference in God-inspired instructions. If we are to know which one is for our participation, we must know where, why, and how to rightly divide.

PETER AND PAUL

Peter was a circumcised, pork-abstaining Jew in Jerusalem when he preached a message of prophetic fulfillment to Israel in Acts 3. Paul was sent to uncircumcised, lobster-eating Gentiles in Greece and Rome (Acts 9:15). Peter and Paul's audiences were different, but there is more than this. The content of their messages was different as well.

Peter presented a message of repentance that was spoken by prophets since the world began (Acts 3:21).

"Yea, and all the prophets from Samuel and those that follow after, as many as have spoken, have likewise foretold of these days."　　　　　　　　　　　　　　–Acts 3:24

Paul's gospel spoke about a mystery of Christ kept secret since the world began, purposed "before the world began" (2 Tim 1:9):

> "Now to him that is of power to stablish you according to my gospel, and the preaching of Jesus Christ, according to the revelation of the mystery, which was kept secret since the world began"   – Romans 16:25

One was spoken; the other was kept secret. Things that are different are not the same.

SEPARATE WHAT IS DIFFERENT

We have easily identified significant differences in Peter and Paul's ministries. It is right to divide what is different. A good place to make a right division in our Bible would be between Peter and Paul (Gal 2:7).

Peter and Paul both taught Jesus Christ. They both taught him as the Son of God. They both witnessed that he had resurrected. They both preached a gospel, exhibited faith, and were promised salvation, but they taught Christ differently: one according to prophecy and the other according to a mystery. One taught prophetic fulfillment to Israel; the other taught a mystery to all men.

Surely, there are elements that are the same throughout the Bible. These themes are important when studying God's eternal purpose (Eph 1:10), but careful students of the Bible cannot overlook the differences in God's progressive revelations.

There is no reason to run from the differences in the Bible. When we identify and separate them, then the Bible will open up. These differences are the key to understanding how to rightly divide the Bible. Right division is necessary to clearly identify which of God's instructions are for our participation and what God is doing in our world today.

CHAPTER 8
RIGHTLY DIVIDING THE LIGHT

The Bible refers to God's word as a light and lamp. When properly used by faith, it enlightens our understanding and guides us into righteousness.

"The entrance of thy words giveth light; it giveth understanding unto the simple. "   – Psalm 119:130

Yet, the Bible remains a dark book for many who find it hard to understand. It is common to find a passage instructing one thing and another instructing a contrary thing. With so many different "lights," the Bible can be confusing. The answer to identifying the right light is to know that God's word is revealed progressively and so must be rightly divided.

It is Satan's strategy to shine all the lights at once to confuse the light of prophecy with the light of the mystery of Christ (2 Cor 11:13-15).

LIGHT GIVEN TO ISRAEL

When God created Israel to be his chosen people, he gave them his law as light from the Lord. As David wrote in the Psalms, the law was a lamp to his feet and a light unto his path (Psa 119:105). It was Israel's responsibility and covenant to be light to the other nations who would come to Zion to learn God's law (Rom 2:19).

"And the Gentiles shall come to thy light, and kings to the brightness of thy rising."
—Isaiah 60:3

"And many people shall go and say, Come ye, and let us go up to the mountain of the LORD, to the house of the God of Jacob; and he will teach us of his ways, and we will walk in his paths: for out of Zion shall go forth the law, and the word of the LORD from Jerusalem."
— Isaiah 2:3

Jesus confirmed Israel's position as a light to the nations in Matthew:

"Ye are the light of the world. A city that is set on an hill cannot be hid."
— Matthew 5:14

WALKING IN ISRAEL'S LIGHT

Walking in Israel's light meant obeying God's law and commandments.

"For the commandment is a lamp; and the law is light;"
— Proverbs 6:23

The way to be in this light of the law and prophets was to do good works.

"But he that doeth truth cometh to the light, that his deeds may be made manifest, that they are wrought in God. "
— John 3:21

If anyone transgressed the law, they were not in the light, but rather, in darkness.

"He that saith he is in the light, and hateth his brother, is in darkness even until now."
— 1 John 2:9

THE GLORIOUS LIGHT OF THE GOSPEL

However, light revealed from God does not end with Israel and prophecy. God had a mystery kept secret until it was revealed to the apostle Paul (1 Cor 2:7-10). Paul's mystery gospel of the glory of the cross is also called light from God:

"For God, who commanded the light to shine out of darkness, hath shined in our hearts, to give the light of the knowledge of the glory of God in the face of Jesus Christ."
— 2 Corinthians 4:6

It was a further revelation of God's will (Eph 1:9-10): that all men could be saved freely by faith alone in the finished work of Christ on the cross. It was to the church that God entrusted this manifold wisdom to enlighten all men to see the fellowship of this mystery (Eph 1:18).

"…to make all men see what is the fellowship of the mystery, which from the beginning of the world hath been hid in God, who created all things by Jesus Christ"
— Ephesians 3:9

WALKING IN THE LIGHT OF GRACE

Since God has revealed his light in the gospel of the mystery of Christ, obedience to the law is no longer walking in the light. Now, walking in the light is walking in the understanding of God's gracious provision of salvation by the cross. We must reckon ourselves dead unto sin and that we are not under the law (Rom 6:11-14).

When we live by faith in Christ according to the mystery, we are living in God's light without the law (Rom 3:21; Rom 8:3-4). The difference is that we are living in the light of the glorious gospel of Christ according to a mystery, not the light of prophecy given to Israel (2 Cor 4:4; Rom 16:25).

"In whom the god of this world hath blinded the minds of them which believe not, lest the light of the glorious gospel of Christ, who is the image of God, should shine unto them."
— 2 Corinthians 4:4

There are many lights in the Bible. Following the wrong one may lead someone away from the gospel of Christ that saves today. Do not think Satan is ignorant of this. It is Satan's strategy to confuse God's word by presenting as many contrary lights as possible (2 Cor 11:13-15). When we rightly divide the light of prophecy from the light of the mystery, we are able to discern God's will and word for us today.

FOR OUR LEARNING

In Paul's God-inspired writings we find the doctrine to the church today. Yet, it would be foolish to say we should eliminate the other parts of scripture.

> "All scripture is given by inspiration of God, and is profitable for doctrine, for reproof, for correction, for instruction in righteousness:"   – 2 Timothy 3:16

Right division does not eliminate other books of the Bible. Instead, it rightly defines their context so that we can have a complete doctrinal understanding. It is all for our learning.

> "For whatsoever things were written aforetime were written for our learning…"   – Romans 15:4

WHAT WE LEARN

With the scriptures written to God's prophetic people, Israel, we learn about God's promised purpose for the earth. He promised to have dominion over the planet from the throne of David. Paul's gospel explains further the mystery behind the resurrection of David's seed (2 Tim 2:8).

We need every page of the Bible to learn about God's character. God is great! He is gracious, just, and true. Learning about his faithfulness encourages us to have hope in what Paul says also (Rom 4:21-23).

"...for our learning, that we through patience and comfort of the scriptures might have hope."   – Romans 15:4
Paul says about the law:

"I had not known sin, but by the law: for I had not known lust, except the law had said, Thou shalt not covet."
– Romans 7:7

OUR HISTORY

Most importantly, God's hidden purpose could not have been accomplished without the necessary preparation by the law and the prophets.

"Wherefore the law was our schoolmaster to bring us unto Christ, that we might be justified by faith."
– Galatians 3:24

"But now the righteousness of God without the law is manifested, being witnessed by the law and the prophets;"
– Romans 3:22

Jesus' mystery message could not have been revealed at any other time in history. God's grace was revealed exactly when it was needed.

FALSE ACCUSERS

Sometimes we who rightly divide are falsely accused of eliminating portions of the Bible because we understand the priority of Jesus' message through Paul over his message through Moses. Yet, dispensational right division does not teach the elimination of any book of scripture but merely their full understanding through Christ's further revelation.

Paul uses the other scriptures repeatedly to teach eternal truths about God, reference Israel's program, and use the law as a schoolmaster. Paul compares and contrasts his revelation from the Lord to the revelation in the law repeatedly. Without the other scriptures, Paul's books would lose their meaning!

Right division requires that we follow Paul if we are to follow Christ, and Paul tells us that we need God's complete revelation for our learning.

ARE MATTHEW, MARK, LUKE, & JOHN OLD TESTAMENT BOOKS?

The New Testament section in the table of contents of every printed Bible begins with the books of Matthew, Mark, Luke, and John[1]. This is not a doctrinal fact, but a result of the publishers' attempt to aid in Biblical division[2]. They are not helping.

---

[1] This is something Bible students should know, but surprisingly most do not. The average Christian and American are Biblically illiterate, only half of which are able to name one of the four gospels. See Prothero, Stephen R. Religious Literacy. [San Francisco]: HarperSanFrancisco, 2007. Print.

[2] The publisher's division reflects the time and language the books of the Bible were inspired. The publisher's Old Testament portion of the printed Bible was inspired among the ancient Hebrews. The publisher's New Testament portion consists of books inspired hundreds of years later to Hebrews living under the Roman Empire. When the books were written is less important for the Bible student than what is written in them.

The doctrinal fact is that the old testament given to Israel does not start until 69 chapters after the publisher's labeled Old Testament[3].

The unwarranted division imposed on the text poses a hindrance for studying the Bible rightly divided. The problem is more evident in the New Testament title page of separation. This page unnecessarily causes many problems in understanding Jesus' earthly ministry to Israel since his entire ministry is actually under the old covenant given to Moses.

Hebrews 9:15-17 explains that the new covenant of Jeremiah 31:31 could be of force only after Jesus died, which is not until the final chapters of Matthew, Mark, Luke, and John.

"And for this cause he is the mediator of the new testament that by means of death, for the redemption of the transgressions that were under the first testament ... For where a testament is, there must also of necessity be the death of a testator. For a testament is of force after men are dead: otherwise it is of no strength at all while the testator liveth."

– Hebrews 9:15-17

Galatians 4:4 explains Jesus lived under the first testament:

"...when the fulness of the time was come, God sent forth his Son, made of a woman, made under the law"

– Galatians 4:4

---

[3] Most Bibles have a page in front of Genesis 1:1 declaring what follows to be the "Old Testament," but the real Mosaic covenant is not given by God until Moses climbs Mt. Sinai in Exodus 19.

The Law of Moses was the old covenant. According to Galatians 4:4, Jesus was born and lived under the old covenant. It was not until his death that the new covenant could be made available. Since the majority of each narrative and the entirety of the Lord's earthly ministry occurred before his death, then it should be considered that these four books are still in the context of the old covenant. This would explain why Paul wrote that Jesus "was a minister of the circumcision to confirm the promises made unto the fathers" (Rom 15:8). This would also explain why Jesus operated according to the old testament:

1. He was circumcised (Luke 2:27)
2. Water baptized (Matt 3:15)
3. Taught conditional forgiveness (Matt 6:14)
4. Taught Levitical sacrifice for healing (Matt 8:4)
5. "Follow the commandments" (Mark 10:17-19)
6. "Obey the Pharisees" (Matt 23:2-3)
7. Observed feast days (Matt 26:17)

Nearly a century ago, Bible teacher J.C. O'Hair mentioned[4] three things that would advance our Bible understanding:

1. The Old Testament does not begin with the first chapter in Genesis.
2. The New Testament does not begin with the first chapter of Matthew.
3. The dispensation of the grace of God does not begin with Peter in Acts 2, but with Paul.

---

[4] O'Hair, J.C. *Unsearchable Riches of Christ*. Grace Publications. Grand Rapids, MI. page 5.

To understand the Bible, the context must be rightly identified, and rightly divided. The events in Matthew, Mark, Luke, and John happened under the old testament. We cannot honestly take those books as our doctrine without placing ourselves in the context of the Old Testament.

THE 2000 YEAR GAP

We now live in a dispensation not prophesied of God and operate according to the mystery of Christ. The current dispensation of grace is found neither in the prophetic schedule written by Daniel nor in the ministry of the Spirit at Pentecost.

In Daniel 9:24, there is a prophetic schedule given of 70 weeks (weeks of years) to finish the prophecy concerning Israel and Jerusalem. Daniel 9:25 says that this 490-year schedule begins at the commandment to restore and to build Jerusalem:

> "Know therefore and understand, that from the going forth of the commandment to restore and to build Jerusalem unto the Messiah the Prince shall be seven weeks, and threescore and two weeks:" – Daniel 9:25

We have another marker after the 69th week that is after 483 years, which tells when the Messiah will be cut off:

> "And after threescore and two weeks shall Messiah be cut off..." – Daniel 9:26

This leaves only 1 week of years (7 years) left on the prophetic timetable of Daniel to seal up the prophecy after Christ's crucifixion at approximately 29 A.D.

DANIEL'S MISSING 70TH WEEK

Misinterpretation of Daniel's 70th week has led many Bible students to think we are now living in the prophesied kingdom or that the numbers in the Bible cannot be literal.

Covenant theologians believe that the 70 weeks were completed at the destruction of Jerusalem in 70 A.D by the Roman Titus. The problem with this view of prophecy is that it leaves a 40-year gap between the 69th and 70th week when there should be only seven.

Acts 2 dispensationalists, recognizing the absence of the prophesied kingdom, correctly identify that there has been an interruption in Daniel's 70-week prophecy. However, the Acts 2 dispensationalist makes a mistake by inserting the dispensational change in Acts 2 at the Jewish Pentecost. This creates another problem in that Peter identifies Acts 2 as the "last days" according to Joel. According to Peter, Daniel's time clock was still ticking.

> "And it shall come to pass in the last days, saith God, I will pour out of my Spirit upon all flesh"   – Acts 2:17

The Acts 2 sending of the Spirit on a Jewish feast day was not the start of something new; it was the last days of prophecy! So then, what explains the two thousand year gap in prophecy from Peter's day until now?

A BIBLE BELIEVING ALTERNATIVE

The gap is not explained in prophecy and as such was a mystery. This is exactly what we find in the revelation from Jesus given to the last apostle, Paul: a revelation of a mystery kept secret.

"I am made a minister, according to the dispensation of God which is given to me for you, to fulfil the word of God; Even the mystery which hath been hid from ages and from generations..." — Colossians 1:25-26

Peter offered Israel an opportunity to repent and usher in the final days of prophecy in Acts 3:19-20. When Israel rejected the apostolic offer of repentance, God revealed a mystery of the gospel to send salvation to Gentiles.

"...rather through their fall salvation is come unto the Gentiles, for to provoke them to jealousy." — Romans 11:11

For the past two thousand years, we have been living in the mystery dispensation of God's grace and peace. Prophecy regarding the fulfillment of prophetic Israel and their holy city is not being fulfilled during this mystery dispensation.

The keystone of our mission today is the preaching of the cross and not the soon coming kingdom, which God postponed until the fulness of the Gentiles be come in (Rom 11:25-26). Prophecy is not yet finished. Israel has not yet received its promised salvation (Rom 11:26-27).

The change occurred neither in Acts 2 nor in 70 A.D. The change occurred in the middle of the book of Acts when Christ chose the chief of sinners to be a new apostle sent to all men preaching Jesus Christ according to the revelation of the mystery. Mid-Acts Pauline dispensational Bible belief is the key to understanding the current dispensational gap in Daniel's prophetic timeline and what God is doing now.

CHAPTER 9
KEEPING A SECRET IN BIBLE STUDY

Once you know a secret it is hard to pretend you do not know it. However, this is exactly what we must do when we study the older scriptures in their context.

Here is an illustration. I was trying to solve a puzzle and spent all my mental effort to reach the solution. Minutes turned to hours, and day after day, I would think about the puzzle and could not figure it out. Then I discovered the secret, and the fog of confusion cleared. The puzzle worked! When I reviewed my thought process, I found that the secret fit every thought. It was as if my mind was circling the answer but could not point it out.

When others were challenged by the puzzle, I thought, "It is so clear!" Yet, they could not see it. It was not that others were unintelligent, but they did not yet know the secret. I could not remove what I knew from my mind, but it had not yet entered theirs. It is the same when studying the Bible.

THEY DID NOT KNOW THE MYSTERY

Now that we have the mystery of Christ revealed, it is easier to see God's eternal purpose throughout all of scripture. We can read it in between the lines, in God's mind, on every page and see it in every step of God's progressive revelation. The law and the prophets encircled the cross, yet not a single prophet understood it. It seems so obvious to us that Christ dying for sins was pictured back in the temple sacrifices. However, since Christ had not yet been revealed, God told the priests that the animals' blood forgave sins.

When God promised forgiveness and blessing to Israel, it is obvious to us that he could not fulfill this promise without Christ. Yet, Abram did not have a clue about the meaning of the Lord's death, burial, and resurrection.

When Jesus first told his chosen twelve apostles that he would die, they were ignorant of what he meant and even tried to prevent it (Mat 16:22).

"And they understood none of these things: and this saying was hid from them, neither knew they the things which were spoken. "   – Luke 18:34

Even after Christ died and the disciples witnessed his resurrection, the mystery of Christ had not yet been revealed. How God could justify ungodly men without the law, apart from Israel, not under a covenant remained a secret. Before the revelation of the mystery, James writes to the twelve tribes of Israel about faith with the law, and does not mention the cross of Christ even once (James 1:1; James 2:24).

THE SECRET IS NOT FOUND BEFORE IT WAS REVEALED

It is easy for us to read the accounts of Matthew-John and insert what we know as the preaching of the cross in between the lines, but we would be wrong. It is not there. When we are reading the past, we must remember that they were ignorant of the mystery and still puzzled. When we consider what they did not know, the reason they walked in circles around the cross becomes apparent. When we wrongly try to follow their ministry example, our preaching hides the cross and becomes a puzzle to those who hear us.

When we study, we must respect that the mystery was hid throughout the law, the prophets, and Jesus' apostolic ministry to Israel, yet now we must communicate the gospel of the mystery of Christ revealed.

FINDING SCRIPTURE THAT APPLIES TO US

The Bible can be unexciting. For an example, try reading 1 Chronicles 1-3 for your devotional this week. There is little room for personal application from the God-inspired words in 1 Chronicles 1:2-3: "Kenan, Mahaleel, Jered, Henoch, Methusaleh, Lamech."

This text is informational, but it does not exactly give you divine insight into the everyday decisions of your life. Likewise, there are passages of the Bible that are apparently not addressed to anyone on the planet today:

"I have called Bezaleel the son of Uri... to devise cunning works, to work in gold, and in silver ... to work in all manner of workmanship."   – Exodus 31:1-5

I am confident that after reading this verse, Bezaleel would come away with a clear sense of God's purpose for his life. Now, what about the rest of us? Proper application of scripture requires us to determine if we fit in the audience of the passage. There are parts of the Bible that are not addressed to us. This is normal.

Reading these sections is like reading someone else's mail. We can learn things about someone else's life, but not about our own. Reading those passages in the Bible tells us about God and his purpose for people in that context but not about his purpose directed to us.

Jesus told his disciples at one time, "Go not into the way of the Gentiles" (Mat 10:6). If Christians applied this literally to their lives, they would be catching the first flight to Jerusalem! It would be wise not to apply these words to your ministerial plans without reading further.

If you are looking to save some time by finding the passages in the Bible addressed to you, then you need to start with Paul. The Lord gave Paul the office of "Apostle of the Gentiles" (Rom 11:13). Paul wrote letters to Gentiles about his dispensation from Jesus Christ, which included salvation, the church, service to God, and the nature of "this present evil world."

1 Chronicles 1 addresses people for whom national genealogy is of religious significance. It is not addressed to us (Titus 3:9). If you are looking for verses to apply to your life that are not addressed to a law-keeping, temple-building, pork-abstaining, nation of Israelites, then look first to Paul's writings.

As C.I. Scofield put it, "In his writings alone we find the doctrine, position, walk, and destiny of the church.[1]" As Paul himself put it, "Consider what I say; and the Lord give thee understanding in all things." (2 Tim 2:7)

THE BIBLE FACT OF DIFFERENT GOSPELS

"No intelligent student of the Scriptures believes, or teaches, that there is only one gospel in the Scriptures…"
– J.C. O'Hair[2]

This statement describing the level of Bible study in the past century would now be considered offensive or shocking to the average Christian. What has diminished is not the truth of O'Hair's statement but the number of intelligent Bible students.

What passes as Bible study today is opening the Bible and applying any verse to our present situation or preaching agenda. Instead of context, they want a proof text. Is there a Bible that proves my agenda? Cursed be the context! Let the facts be gone! If any work is put into this form of foolish Bible practice it is in twisting the verse out of its context and spinning it to meet a particular belief system or thought.

---

[1] This statement is found in the note on Ephesians 3:6 in the old Scofield Reference Bible.
[2] O'Hair, J.C. *Unsearchable Riches of Christ*. Grace Publications. Grand Rapids, MI. page 131.

INTELLIGENT BIBLE STUDY

Intelligent Bible study requires collecting the facts of scripture and then letting the context make connections. Interpretation and application come after the collecting of facts. Depending on the facts of the matter, there may be little personal application of passages where we are not in the context. No intelligent student of the Scripture would refuse to hear the facts before making an interpretation or application.

The facts are that the gospel of the kingdom and the gospel of the grace of God are different messages. There is no deep interpretation to this conclusion; it requires only fact collection.

Fact #1: The gospel Paul preached includes Christ dying for our sins, his burial, and resurrection.

"I declare unto you the gospel which I preached unto you … By which also ye are saved. … how that Christ died for our sins according to the scriptures; And that he was buried, and that he rose again the third day according to the scriptures"   – 1 Corinthians 15:1-4

Fact #2: Christ sent his disciples to preach the gospel of the kingdom.

"Then he called his twelve disciples together, and gave them power and authority over all devils, and to cure diseases. And he sent them to preach the kingdom of God, and to heal the sick…And they departed, and went through the towns, preaching the gospel, and healing every where." – Luke 9:1-6

Fact #3: The twelve disciples did not understand the death, burial, and resurrection of Christ while they were preaching the gospel of the kingdom.

"Then he took unto him the twelve, and said unto them, Behold, we go up to Jerusalem, and all things that are written by the prophets concerning the Son of man shall be accomplished. For he shall be delivered unto the Gentiles, and shall be mocked, and spitefully entreated, and spitted on: And they shall scourge him, and put him to death: and the third day he shall rise again. And they understood none of these things: and this saying was hid from them, neither knew they the things which were spoken." — Luke 18:31-34

Conclusion #1 (based on the facts): The gospel of the kingdom and Paul's gospel are different messages.

There is zero room for interpretation and zero application in this conclusion, and yet, it is rejected, if not considered extremely offensive, by a majority of Christians in the 21st century.

Conclusion #2: Christians in the 21st century are unaware of Bible facts regarding the gospels.

Intelligent Bible study collects the facts first. Intelligent Bible study will lead to a confrontation with mid-Acts Pauline dispensational right division. No intelligent student of the Scriptures believes, or teaches, that there is only one gospel in the Scriptures. The facts bear this out. No interpretation is needed. If anyone says otherwise, then there is good reason to doubt their ability to study or their intelligence. Let the dumb be dumb. Let the facts speak!

THE MANY GOSPELS OF THE BIBLE

Although every man at any time is saved by the grace of God through faith, the content of faith differs from one dispensation to the next. That is, the message that is offered and believed for righteousness and salvation varies according to God's progressive revelation. These different gospel messages can be understood when we carefully study what God had revealed, when, and to whom.

NOAH AND RIGHTEOUSNESS

In Genesis, Noah was counted righteous because of his obedience by faith toward God. He and his family were saved through building an ark in a world without rain. His faith and obedience was not based upon the knowledge of the death and resurrection of Jesus Christ, but in the living God and his promise of a flood.

> "By faith Noah, being warned of God of things not seen as yet, moved with fear, prepared an ark to the saving of his house; by the which he condemned the world, and became heir of the righteousness which is by faith."
>
> – Hebrews 11:7

While Peter explains that Noah's salvation was a figure of the salvation found in the resurrection of Christ, there is no mention of Noah's understanding of this truth. Peter reveals that no prophet understood such a salvation through Christ until after his death:

> "Of which salvation the prophets have enquired and searched diligently, who prophesied of the grace that should come unto you: Searching what, or what manner of time the Spirit of Christ which was in them did signify, when it testified beforehand the sufferings of Christ, and the glory that should follow."   – 1 Peter 1:10-11

ABRAM AND RIGHTEOUSNESS

It cannot be ignored that Abram was counted righteous because of his faith in God's promise of a mighty nation, not the death and resurrection of Jesus Christ (Genesis 15:6). We now know that sinful Abram could be justified without works because of the then future, propitiatory work of Christ, but Abram did not know that. The word of faith that he believed was the promise of a land, seed, and blessing. As Paul explains, Abraham was "strong in faith" (Rom 4:20).

> "And being fully persuaded that, what he had promised, he was able also to perform. "   – Romans 4:21

The specific promise that God made to Abraham was not that a messiah would die for his sins but that his wife would produce a son though she was barren and beyond her age:

> "Who against hope believed in hope, that he might become the father of many nations, according to that which was spoken, So shall thy seed be." – Romans 4:18

MOSES AND RIGHTEOUSNESS

While Moses was able to have personal conversation with God, he wrote about a righteousness gained from the obedience of faith in the law:

> "And it shall be our righteousness, if we observe to do all these commandments before the LORD our God, as he hath commanded us."   – Deuteronomy 6:25

Paul expounds upon the understanding of Moses when he quotes Leviticus 18:5:

> "For Moses describeth the righteousness which is of the law, That the man which doeth those things shall live by them."   – Romans 10:5

This righteousness and the faith that Moses and his followers had in God's covenant was not faith in the death and resurrection of Jesus Christ (Rom 10:2-9). Their faith in God and his law required obedience. The requirement to do works was a product of the content of their faith in God's revealed covenant.

JOHN THE BAPTIST AND RIGHTEOUSNESS

After a four-century silence in God's plan with Israel, John the Baptist appears on the scene preaching the baptism of repentance for the remission of sins (Mark 1:4). The message he taught was the soon coming of the promised kingdom to Israel and the Messiah. Once again the content of faith was changing. Those who believed his message accepted his baptism. Those who were unfaithful to God's promises rejected his message of faith.

> "But when he saw many of the Pharisees and Sadducees come to his baptism, he said unto them, O generation of vipers, who hath warned you to flee from the wrath to come?"
> – Matthew 3:7

The result of accepting John's baptism was a remission of sins and righteousness by the obedience of faith. Jesus demonstrated this by taking part in the baptism, although John declared that he did not need it:

> "But John forbad him, saying, I have need to be baptized of thee, and comest thou to me? And Jesus answering said unto him, Suffer it to be so now: for thus it becometh us to fulfil all righteousness. Then he suffered him. "
> – Matthew 3:14-15

JESUS AND RIGHTEOUSNESS

During his earthly ministry, Jesus also taught the gospel of the kingdom as John did:

> "Jesus came into Galilee, preaching the gospel of the kingdom of God, And saying, The time is fulfilled, and the kingdom of God is at hand: repent ye, and believe the gospel."
> – Mark 1:14-15

However, Jesus additionally taught the righteousness of the new covenant law.

"Think not that I am come to destroy the law, or the prophets: I am not come to destroy, but to fulfil."

– Matthew 5:17

"For I say unto you, That except your righteousness shall exceed the righteousness of the scribes and Pharisees, ye shall in no case enter into the kingdom of heaven."

–Matthew 5:20

Although this standard of righteousness seemed to be stringent, they were promised the power of the Holy Ghost to help, and there were abundant rewards for those who "endured to the end" (Matt 10:22).

"But seek ye first the kingdom of God, and his righteousness; and all these things shall be added unto you."

– Matthew 6:33

It should be noted that even though Jesus taught the law, coming kingdom, and his identity as the Son of God, belief in his atoning death and resurrection was not the gospel message offered for righteousness or salvation during his earthly ministry. In fact, when he did try to explain to his disciples that he had to die, they were ignorant of the matter, and the Lord let them be ignorant:

"And they understood none of these things: and this saying was hid from them, neither knew they the things which were spoken. "   – Luke 18:34

THE DISCIPLES & THE NEW COVENANT OF RIGHTEOUSNESS

After the institution of the New Covenant and empowerment by the Holy Ghost, Peter and John wrote about a faith in Jesus as the Messiah and his resurrection. Peter explains that remaining faithful to God and his Son through the immediate trials of tribulation would secure salvation and righteousness for believers in the end:

"That the trial of your faith, being much more precious than of gold that perisheth, though it be tried with fire, might be found unto praise and honour and glory at the appearing of Jesus Christ: ... Receiving the end of your faith, even the salvation of your souls."   – 1 Peter 1:7, 9

The content of the faith that they had to believe was preached by Peter at his Pentecostal debut:

"Therefore let all the house of Israel know assuredly, that God hath made that same Jesus, whom ye have crucified, both Lord and Christ."   – Acts 2:36

John also writes that their faith rested in the message that Jesus was indeed the Son of God, the promised Messiah.

"But these are written, that ye might believe that Jesus is the Christ, the Son of God; and that believing ye might have life through his name. "   –John 20:31

"Whosoever believeth that Jesus is the Christ is born of God: and every one that loveth him that begat loveth him also that is begotten of him."   – 1 John 5:1

"He that hath the Son hath life; and he that hath not the Son of God hath not life. "   – 1 John 5:12

"If ye know that he is righteous, ye know that every one that doeth righteousness is born of him."   –1 John 2:29

This message of faith in the name of Jesus as Christ and Messiah was essential to entering the kingdom and receiving the salvation that God had promised.

CONCLUSION

Listed here is a simple summary of different gospels found in the Bible. It is not exhaustive. It does not include the glorious gospel of grace revealed by Christ to Paul. However, this short list is sufficient to see that there were separate messages[3] offered for righteousness and salvation as God's word was progressively revealed.

The message we preach for faith today is in the finished work of Christ, the grace of God. God justifies freely those that believe (Romans 3:24-25; Romans 4:5). Our faith is not accompanied by our work, because our faith is in the finished work of Christ.

Paul says that in his gospel is the righteousness of God revealed from faith to faith. Men are always saved by God's grace through faith. The content of faith is what changes and with it the required response. The man of faith obeys. The Bible tells of many men of faith, but what they knew and believed was different.

---

[3] The message was different, but the means of salvation has always been the same. Salvation can only ever be by God's grace through faith. The content of their faith is what changed as God revealed his will.

Only when God's word is rightly divided can we understand the different gospels and changing requirements in the Bible as the just sought the righteousness of God by faith in what God revealed to them.

"For therein is the righteousness of God revealed from faith to faith: as it is written, The just shall live by faith."

– Romans 1:17

Part IV

DOING THE WORK

"All scripture is given by inspiration of God, and is profitable for doctrine, for reproof, for correction, for instruction in righteousness: that the man of God may be perfect, throughly furnished unto all good works."
-2 Timothy 3:16-17

CHAPTER 10

How to Study

Perhaps no one has shown you how to study the Bible. Here are the steps:

1) Read it, and read it again (Rom 10:17). You will not know God or his words without reading them. Start doing this immediately. You must become familiar.

2) Compare similar verses (1 Cor 2:13). Use an electronic concordance to find every other verse with similar words in seconds. You can also use a printed concordance. You can also search for related words. Compare scripture with scripture.

3) Determine the application (Neh 8:8)[1]. This is what we call right division. Not every verse in the Bible was written to you. You must determine who is speaking and where it fits in God's purpose. Was it for Israel? Is it for the church today? This is where the confusion lies within the church. You must become fully persuaded in your own mind (Rom 14:5).

---

[1] The priests in Nehemiah 8:8 "gave the sense" of the scriptures and "caused them to understand the law."

Only you can do the first step. There are tools to help with the second[2]. This book and our websites are designed to help you with the third[3].

This method of studying can be called exegetical. This is because you are trying to explain what you just read from scripture. Another way of Bible study is called topical Bible study. The only difference is the first step.

1) Choose a topic, or ask a question.

2) Compare verses with a concordance search using words related to the topic.

3) Determine the application.

Using topical studies are good for showing God's changing dispensational instructions. Try studying God's dietary instructions or how God grants forgiveness.

At our fellowship we have separate meetings for exegetical and topical studies. As you study you will see your faith increase, and your discernment will grow. If you do not, you are doing something wrong. Contact us via our website (see footnote below) for help.

DOCTRINAL STUDY IS SPECIFIC

Christians have become specialists in extracting the useful spiritual truth from the Bible.

"All the Bible is useful for us!" they say.

---

[2] These tools were mentioned in chapter 2.
[3] Along with printed materials offered by AmbassorsPublishing.com, GraceAmbassadors.com has thousands of free resources, audios, outlines, and commentary on the Bible rightly divided.

This is true, but not specifically, not practically. For the Bible to become specifically useful, we need to understand the context of a passage. Doctrinal Bible study creates the context of a passage. It answers who is speaking, to whom, and are we in the audience? The doctrine gives each verse a specific purpose.

Using spiritual truths without respecting the doctrinal context leads to Bible verses being used for wrong purposes and out of context. Ignoring specific doctrinal study leads to a message that sounds good but simply does not work all the time. If you want to know the specific purpose and will of God, then study the Bible doctrinally. You will find God's specific purpose in the context.

PAUL'S CURRICULUM

It is true that in Paul's epistles alone we find the doctrine, walk, destiny, and purpose of the church for this dispensation. Paul's epistles reveal a spiritual curriculum to produce unashamed workmen fit for God's service.

Doctrine	Reproof	Correction
Romans	Corinthians	Galatians
Ephesians	Philippians	Colossians
Thessalonians		
Instruction in Righteousness		
Timothy	Titus	Philemon

We can see this curriculum arranged according to the four points of profit in 2 Timothy 3:16 that make "the man of God perfect, throughly furnished unto all good works" (2 Tim 3:17).

Of course, all scripture profits in these four ways, but it is interesting to see how each epistle Paul writes seems to fit generally into one of the four profit categories.

Below are brief summaries of Paul's epistles in their canonical order.

- **Romans:** Laying a doctrinal foundation; instilling right doctrine
- **Corinthians:** Producing good works under grace; moving people to act
- **Galatians:** Walking in the Spirit, not under law
- **Ephesians:** The nature and mission of the church
- **Philippians:** The mind of Christ; instruction in maturity
- **Colossians:** Operating complete in Christ
- **Thessalonians:** Comfort and hope waiting for the return of the Lord
- **1 Timothy/ Titus:** Teaching and leadership instructions
- **Philemon:** Paul's example of charity
- **2 Timothy:** Final words for faithful men

You can see the natural doctrinal progression as you read through Paul's epistles that ends with the man of God being throughly furnished (2 Timothy 3:17). Every book fits somewhere in the Pauline curriculum. Not very many finish the course. Identify where you are in your growth, and start your study there. Don't know where you are? Start at the beginning. Do not quit, and you will be able to teach others also (2 Tim 2:2).

STUDY LARGE PASSAGES

Do you have studies with a spouse or a group? Are you studying a large book? Do you quit after a few weeks because the study does not ever seem to finish? Try studying larger portions in each study. The study will be more consistent with the context of the book and will help you grasp a better understanding of the important doctrines.

You can come back later and study the details on your own. If your study is once a week, try one whole chapter a week. Skim and summarize. That will take four months through Romans. Still too long? Try three chapters in one session a week. Sometimes the "trouble" passages are just one or two verses that may not change the context. Get a bird's eye view and move on.

In our dispensational chart lessons we cover 1,200 chapters in one hour. It is useful for people who still need an introduction to the material. If you lead the study, it will be helpful for you since there is less you need to know about the details: just the highlights, then move on.

CHOOSE ONE OF 66

Reading through the entire Bible is important. Many people have not read it once. Sometimes making smaller goals can help. If you have been struggling to get through the entire Bible for years, try cutting yourself some slack. Choose one book and master it. Instead of knowing a little about sixty-six books, know a lot about one book. This is not the end goal, but it will reap more benefits than failing to get past Exodus every January.

Read your one book as many times as you can. Outline it. Analyze it. Studying the questions raised from just one book will force you through many others. I would choose one of Paul's (they are shorter).

66 BOOK STUDIES

Every Tuesday night our church meets to do verse-by-verse, expositional Bible study. Verse-by-verse is like writing a commentary. It is very slow work. At the pace we are going, I will not finish the whole Bible verse-by-verse in my lifetime. Praise God that people are studying the Bible on their own... right?

Every Christian should do a simple book study of all 66 books of the Bible. A book study is not verse-by-verse commentary. A book study requires enough familiarity with the book to know what it is about, to know what the important passages are, and to create a general outline.

Producing 66 book studies should take less than 5 years during normal Bible study time each week. Children should be required to do this by their parents. This is not busy work or school homework that will be trashed upon graduation. This is a good start for a lifetime of Bible study. By the time they get their first job they will have done two things many Christians have not done. 1) read through the entire Bible; 2) provide a summary of each book.

The first lesson of every new book we study verse-by-verse is a general summary of the book. Take our "Introduction" outlines as a pattern[4]. Before you can rightly divide, you must know what needs dividing.

---

[4] www.graceambassadors.com/verse

MAKE YOUR OWN TABLE OF CONTENTS

Before I read a book, I always read the table of contents. A good table of contents acts as a summary of ideas for each chapter and can show the flow of ideas through the book. This prepares my mind to read the book in detail, alerting me what to expect and to sections I can skim or skip altogether. While reading, I can always go back and consult the table of contents to get a bird's eye view of where I am in the book.

Most table of contents in Bibles are minimal and do not contain much helpful information about the content of books. Publishers do this to remain doctrinally neutral. Your study of the Bible should not be doctrinally neutral: make your own table of contents.

Understanding the timeline of the Bible, the flow of ideas presented, and how God intervenes from beginning to end can help in your daily reading. This is why half a dozen times each year I teach a timeline of the Bible on Sunday mornings. These repetitive summary lessons build a proper table of contents in our minds.

Accompanying these "table of contents" lessons is often a drawing or chart of the Bible. Such a timeline would be very useful in the beginning of your Bible next to the table of contents. I have produced such a dispensational chart that easily fits in the front cover of your Bible. You can get one online[5].

---

[5] www.dispensationalchart.com

Learn By Summarizing

Summarizing can simplify what you read. It gives you a big picture. To understand better the themes and doctrines throughout the Bible, summarize. I do not mean summarize each book. Rather, summarize the entire book. If you need to skip some prophets and most of the law, then fine. The goal is to explain the teaching of the entire Bible in a way that is easy to understand.

Make sure you explain the major changes in God's dealing with humanity. Mention some events that are commonly understood from Genesis to Revelation. Doing this will help you bring it all together. If you can do it in less than 5-10 minutes then you are ready to explain the Bible to others who do not read it. You do not need to know every detail of Zephaniah before you have a general understanding. Start big.

Replace your daily Bible reading this week with this big picture exercise. It will help you understand the Bible.

Write Your Own Commentary

Have you started your own commentary yet? It is easy and helps your understanding. As you read through a passage, journal as if you are explaining the verses to someone else. Write as if you are trying to explain it to a 10-year-old child. Children are smart but do not suffer lofty, sanctimonious writing. You do not want to sound like a dusty scholar.

If you get to a part that is a little confusing, resist the temptation to look at another commentary. Use your own thoughts. Write your own words. Make a list of cross-references and external sources. After you have written your thoughts, then check another commentary. Does it line up? Should it line up? Remember commentaries are just another man's thoughts.

What you are doing is establishing a record of your understanding of God's word. You can refer to it later if you forget. Your children can use it as a reference, and your grandchildren will see it as a treasure.

Teachers have long known that explaining to other people is the best way to learn. Use this technique to your spiritual advantage – start a commentary!

CREATING CROSS REFERENCES

As you study the Bible from the perspective of the mystery of Christ revealed first to Paul, you begin to see connections that no other Bible or commentary has in print. You will need to create your own cross references where none existed and reevaluate references that are no longer valid as they wrongly connect verses that need divided.

Popular reference lists love to cross-reference 1 Corinthians 12:13 with Pentecost in Acts 2. We know better[6]. Another troublesome example may be with the "law of liberty" in James that most printed Bibles will reference to one of Paul's epistles. Knowing that James was written to the remnant of Israel under the law, we know that a better reference would be to Psalm 119:44-45.

---

[6] 1 Corinthians 12:13 is talking about our baptism into one body, the mystery church called a new creature (2 Cor 5:17). Acts 2 records the pouring out of the Holy Ghost on Jews in an upper room in preparation for the coming kingdom as spoken by the prophets. One was a mystery, and the other was prophesied. They are not the same.

MARGINAL NOTES

There are not many books written about the Bible from a mid-Acts dispensational perspective. For most of the books I read, I must carefully find the meat and spit out the bones. (I do a lot of spitting.)

To help in identifying problem areas in a book, I write simple codes in the margin. Here are a few of my most used:

- **P/M** – Used when the author fails to rightly divide prophecy from mystery. (This is common.)
- **OC** – Used for when the author uses scripture out of its context.
- **DI**(sp) – Used when the author thinks the entire Bible is for our participation. They do not distinguish dispensations.
- **TR** – Used when the author attacks my translation, or makes weak arguments based on "a better translation would be."

This practice helps to analyze the content as I am reading it and helps to identify the bones clearly. It is sad to see how a failure to rightly divide produces so many wrong conclusions. When there are too many problems in the margin, I put the book down. It has too many bones, and there is a good chance it will be a waste of time to continue, or worse, make me choke.

If you do not like to write in your books, then download an electronic version and attach your notes digitally. This way your notes are searchable on your computer.

Staying in the margins will help you from falling into the errors of the mainstream.

DISCOVERING THE DEEP THINGS

The "deep things of God" (1 Cor 2:10) are revealed in the scripture by the Spirit. There is not a mystical secret, technique, or crystal ball to unveil hidden wisdom from another spiritual dimension. The hidden wisdom, which is the mystery of Christ (1 Cor 2:6-8), has been written down for us with words in the Bible.

When you read Paul's letters, you are reading the words the Holy Ghost moved Paul to write (2 Tim 3:16). They are God's words (1 Thess 2:13). They are the only words from God you will receive this side of eternity.

Sometimes people think God gives certain people secret knowledge that no one else can access. This is not true. All of God's revelations can be learned by anyone with a Bible who believes it and studies it. The secret ingredient is not special giftings, relaxation techniques, or contemplative prayers. It is study, reading, repetition, and comparing scripture with scripture. Some people are better students than others are, but that does not change what we all study: a book.

It is only through the hard work of Bible study, and that rightly divided, that the deep things of God are known. Do not believe any fool who tells you that learning the deep things of God does not require the effort of studying the Bible.

KNOW YOUR MOTIVATION

What is your motivation for studying the Bible? For some, it is purely academic. Others do it out of habit. Maybe you do it because it is what you are "supposed to do." If you find that Bible study is dry, boring, or fruitless, then perhaps it is a matter of the heart. Jesus taught Israel about their heart priorities. He said where their treasure was their heart would be also.

To get motivated you have to readjust your priorities. If you received fifty dollars every time you studied the book, it would quickly become a priority. Yet how much more valuable is putting on Christ, renewing the inner man, experiencing peace, and producing good works?

You have the opportunity to reap greater riches from the Bible than anyone throughout history (Eph 3:8)! When you see the value of sound Bible study then you are willing to invest in it. Remember this when you start to feel bored with study.

CHAPTER 11
BIBLE STUDY TIPS

TIP #1: START OVER

Have you learned to rightly divide after years of studying the Bible? It is time to start over. Reread the Bible. You may have been painting a picture of what the Bible says for years, but you have now changed your perspective on the subject. You need a new canvas.

You will need to study each book again from the perspective of the Bible rightly divided. You will be amazed at how different they look now that you are standing in a different position about Prophecy and Mystery. Phrases and words in the Psalms will jump out at you regarding Israel's earthly kingdom. The historical books will no longer be mere stories but will be material repeated in Jesus' earthly ministry.

By learning right division you will need to unlearn other things. It may call into question some previously held beliefs. Learning to rightly divide is not just some new doctrine to add to your existing repertoire, it is a change in perspective. It will change how you see everything in the Bible.

TIP #2: RECREATE THE WHEEL

I have told you before about some amazing free resources accessible on the internet that at one time cost thousands of dollars to purchase. But with access to more information than ever before, there is a tendency not to do personal study. Some studies suggest that our brain changes the way it thinks after prolonged internet use. "Googling" and reading news feeds replaces the age-old task of remembering. The fact that we have genius technology does not mean we live in a society of geniuses.

Sometimes we need to recreate the wheel for the sake of personal growth. Listening through hundreds of sermons does not mean you have studied it yourself. You have only listened to someone else's study. Access to libraries of books does not mean you understand anything in them. Study on your own. Create your own Bible lessons. Outline books, read books, redraw chronologies, create lists of kings and judges. Draw your own maps. Teach someone. If you spend the time to recreate the wheel, the better chance you will understand how it works.

TIP #3: KNOW THE AUDIENCE

An important part of rightly dividing the Bible is knowing the audience. Before hastily applying doctrine to yourself, ask, "Who is the audience?" Then follow it up with, "Am I in the audience?" If you are not the audience, then the doctrine cannot be applied to you. You can learn from it, but should not live in it. Many books of the Bible reveal the audience in the first few verses.

For example, Obadiah says, "The vision of Obadiah. Thus saith the Lord GOD concerning Edom" (Oba 1:1). Since the Lord is speaking about Edom we do not apply the doctrine of Obadiah to ourselves. Malachi 1:1 says, "The burden of the word of the LORD to Israel by Malachi." Since the LORD is talking to Israel, we do not assume the doctrine of Malachi either. These books are easily discerned and most would agree about their audience.

Here is another example for you to discern on your own as homework. Who is the audience of this book? Are you the audience? Does the doctrine apply to you?

"James, a servant of God and of the Lord Jesus Christ, to the twelve tribes which are scattered abroad, greeting.
– James 1:1

TIP #4: LEAVE CONTRADICTIONS ALONE

Popular teachers of Bible interpretation say that nothing in the Bible can contradict because God cannot contradict himself. So, when students find a contradiction in the Bible, they distort the plain meaning in order to make it align with the doctrine in the rest of the Bible. What a mistake!

The result is one cohesive doctrine taught throughout the Bible at the expense of context and progressive revelation. The truth is that there are statements and even doctrines in the Bible that contradict each other when taken out of context. This does not mean that God is contradictory or illogical.

The answer is as simple as discerning the context: my wife receives different instructions than my mechanic. I do not contradict myself. God does not contradict himself, but he does give different doctrines to people that are under law and under grace. This is a dispensational difference.

TIP #5: STOP CORRECTING THE BIBLE

Bible correcting is not Bible study. When textual critics and Greek scholars study translation and ancient languages, they are not involved in doctrinal study. Your spiritual growth depends not on your study of Bible translation but on studying the doctrine within the Bible. When you trust the translation, then you have made the conscious choice that the Bible does not need corrected. This will force you to study the meaning of the words and their context instead of looking for a scapegoat through "mistranslation." You are free to study without doubt!

The moment you make this decision, your love for study will change. Your understanding will increase, and your life will start to stabilize on a stronger foundation. Stop correcting and start studying.

TIP #6: BEGIN WITH ROMANS

Are you new to studying the Bible rightly divided? Are you new to leading a Bible study? Consider starting where Paul started with the first saved Gentiles. Study the book of Romans. In it are the foundational doctrines of salvation, Jesus Christ, grace living, progressive revelation, and spiritual maturity. It has what you need to become stable in this dispensation. This is what is meant by the word "stablish" in Romans 16:25. It is also the "spiritual gift" of Romans 1:11, not some sort of tongue talking.

TIP #7: MAKE YOUR OWN LIST OF KINGS

One important tool for studying the prophets is a timeline of the kings of Israel and Judah. Without knowing the time and circumstances of the reign of the kings, it is harder to study the prophecies in their context.

Did you know many prophets lived around the same time? In addition, the prophecies are not always recorded in chronological order. For example Jeremiah 32 is dated as the 10th year of king Zedekiah (Jer 32:1), but later in chapter 36 a word comes in the days of king Jehoiakim (Jer 36:1). If you have made a list of kings, you will notice that these chapters are not chronological: Zedekiah came after Jehoiakim.

There are plenty of free lists available to reference online, but it is always better to start making your own. Making your own list helps you to learn the context of each king's rise to power, whether they were good or bad, the length of their reign, and the circumstances surrounding their death. It is tedious work, but once you have done it, it is finished.

Another good reason to make your own list is that many lists claim that the Bible has mistakes because they cannot reconcile some of the dates. The Bible is not wrong. There are solutions: make your own list.

There are multiple Jehorams, Ahaziahs, and at one point there are three or four kings reigning in the same year. The Bible is known as having some of the most accurate historical listings of ancient kings in the world.

Start making your lists by skimming through the book of the Kings and Chronicles. Do not forget to add the prophets where appropriate.

TIP #8: TIMING PHRASES

The timing of events in the Bible is important for understanding the context. It is important to watch for timing words and phrases that can help us locate events on the timeline of God's progressive revelation. Such phrases include "immediately," "and then," "but now," "after," "henceforth," etc.

Galatians 1:18 tells us that it was at least three years before Paul went to Jerusalem. Acts 9:19-26 has only seven short verses between Paul's conversion and his first Jerusalem visit. Some consider this a contradiction, but phrases that indicate timing help us align the verses.

For example, Acts 9:19 says that Paul was "certain days" with the disciples. How many days? We do not know. Acts 9:22 says, "Saul increased" which would require a passage of time. Acts 9:23 says "after that many days" which speaks to another indeterminate span of time. When people read Acts 9 ignoring the timing phrases it appears that Galatians 1:18 is a contradiction, but when the timing phrases are considered, there is more than enough room in seven verses for three or more years.

TIP #9: STUDY ENGLISH GRAMMAR

In 21st century America, it is easy to assume that we live in a literate nation. The truth is there are still people who cannot read and many of the rest do not read well. Your study of the Bible will be greatly improved if you study the basic elements of English grammar.

Do you know how to find the subject and predicate of a sentence? Do you know the purpose of prepositions? Do you know the function of an adverb?

With a wealth of internet resources, it is easy to find simple, free lessons online. Can't understand a verse? Do not go to a foreign language for light. Learn your own language. Learn to read English. Knowing what words do in a sentence can help you understand a difficult passage.

TIP #10: CAPITALIZATIONS IN THE BIBLE

More than a few people have had questions about the capitalizations of Spirit in the King James Bible. Capitalization conventions are different in other languages. They are absent in some languages including languages the Bible comes from. Their primary function in English is to ease the use of reading and not to change the meaning of words.

Capitalization of nouns and pronouns used for God are called reverential capitals. The word "spirit" is a noun. It can refer to any spirit including God's, or it can refer to God himself as the "Holy Spirit."

You can determine if the noun refers to God by cross-references and context (e.g., Joel 2:28 prophesies about God the Spirit according to Acts 2:17 even though it is lowercased).

Should we trust the capital letters in the Bible? Yes (e.g., Romans 8:16 uses both "spirit" and "Spirit" in one verse). Must we capitalize every word that is ever associated with God? No (e.g., most often the "H" in Holy Spirit is lowercased in the Bible because it is an adjective).

Capitalizations are helpful but are not the nails that form your belief system. A capital letter should not be the only evidence for an interpretation of a word.

TIP #11: NEW DOCTRINE BY RETRANSLATION

There are plenty of false doctrines floating around Christianity that will waste your time. If you can see the smoke, it will be easier to avoid the fire. For example, when a doctrine can be taught only if the Bible is retranslated, then turn around and walk away. You do not want to be burnt by these false teachings.

These doctrines are easy to spot because normally, there are clear Bible verses contrary to them. If you know your Bible, you will immediately try to respond with a clear contrary verse. However, the false teacher expects this response because his doctrine depends upon retranslating the Bible to match his hidden teaching.

His response will be, "That is translated wrong," or, "It's a mistranslation," or, "It's a mistake," and then he will retranslate the verse to say the opposite of your Bible. When you see this happening scream "fire" and run! Anything can be taught from the Bible if we change enough words. I would not trust a man's doctrine that does not respect God to preserve his words. Right doctrine will never require you to sacrifice your Bible.

TIP #12: SINGLE VERSE DOCTRINES

Here is another tip to identify false doctrines that will waste your time. If there is only one verse in all of God's word that can support a teaching, take two steps back.

The Bible has 31,102 verses. The most important truths have more than one verse explaining them. If someone defends a doctrine dogmatically that only has one verse for support, it is time to move on. Either the doctrine is wrong and not from the Bible, or it does not deserve such a dogmatic defense.

In both cases, you are wise to avoid the one giving the dogmatic defense. Bible study for them is not comparing all 31,102 verses. It is finding a single verse and squeezing it until it bleeds. They cannot discern the potential destruction caused by twisting a single verse the wrong way. Many people have been destroyed by zealous teachers of false doctrine that are built upon a single, obscure verse. If it can only be taught from one verse, do not make it a life-changing doctrine, nor trust those who do.

TIP #13: USE PROPER JUDGMENT

It takes good judgment to study the Bible well.

Do not judge a book by its cover. King James did not translate a single word of the King James Bible.

Do not judge a book by its title. Most Bibles have Paul's name in the title of Hebrews, but it just ain't so.

Do not judge a book by its place in the table of contents. The New Testament does not begin with Matthew. The Old Testament does not begin with Genesis, and we are in neither testament.

Do not judge a book by the commentators' notes. Nobody knows for certain when some books were written, and most commentaries fail to rightly divide anyway.

Do not judge a book by its chapter and verse divisions. They were added much later.

Do judge a book by reading the inspired words in it and making a determination about who is speaking, to whom they are speaking, and whether the audience is the church, the Body of Christ or someone else.

TIP #14: DEFINING HARD PHRASES

Everyone finds phrases they do not understand in the Bible. Word definitions can be found in context or dictionaries, but phrases are not found in dictionaries. The wrong thing to do is throw your Bible away and find another translation that says something you understand.

The problem with this is that the paraphrased translation does not explain anything. It only waters down the phrase, sometimes to a point of oversimplification. You may be losing an important nuance for the sake of simplification. If you cannot learn from the context what the phrase means, it is better to use the King James Bible and check commentaries or Bible dictionaries for help on the meaning of hard phrases, idioms, figures of speech, etc.

While commentaries are doctrinally biased and merely men's opinions, they will explain more than a different translation ever could. There is a place for commentaries: it is to get a studied comment on hard Biblical phrases or idioms. Don't throw away the translation; get an explanation. Once you gather a meaning, go back to your Bible to learn what it is teaching. Do not depend on the commentary to tell you what the Bible says rightly divided, they won't know how.

Tip #15: Interpret Using the Easy Verses

When interpreting the Bible, there are easy passages and there are difficult passages. The difficult passages are difficult for everyone, even self-proclaimed scholars. Misinterpreting these passages can create some very strange and dangerous doctrines. Always follow this rule:

Rule: An easier passage overrules a more difficult one.

For some reason, it is common for Bible students to reinterpret the easy passages to match their strained interpretation of a much harder one. This leads to error. Avoid this.

I know a sister who was stuck for years in a Pentecostal environment. This simple rule saved her from ruin. She did not understand the teaching of tongues and Spirit filling, but she understood the clear teaching of Colossians 2:10. This kept her from falling off the deep end. Now, she can rightly divide.

Right division makes some difficult passages easier, but there are still difficult passages. Do not start with these passages. Start with the easy ones; study them deep and long. Mastering the easy passages will profit you more in the end. Make them your foundation. They will protect you from wandering into the dangers of misinterpretation. Master Romans 5:8-10, Ephesians 2:8-10, & Colossians 2:8-10.

Tip #16: Interpret the Hard by the Easy

The Bible contains both easy and hard to understand passages. The easier passages are immediately clear and their understanding is natural. Others require more thought, but are understandable when studied carefully with the context and other similar verses. Then, there are hard passages which seem out of place, contrary to the context, or that speak of things otherwise absent from the Bible. These verses may have multiple possible interpretations, and the audience is often unclear.

The variety of explanations given by "the experts" testifies to the difficulty of these passages for everyone. It is not just you; they are hard for everybody.

There seems to be an attraction to solve these difficult passages and to do so by sacrificing the easy verses on the altar of having an answer. Resist this temptation. These difficult passages are the most dangerous and must be treated with extreme caution. Used wrongly, these verses have the potential to poison someone's entire belief system. Sometimes it is better not to have an answer at all than to have a bad answer.

Never change the clear and simple meaning of an easy verse for the sake of better understanding a hard verse. Always interpret the hard passages by the easy ones.

TIP #17: LEARN TO USE A CONCORDANCE

Where is that verse about "communion?" Do you know all the verses in the Bible using the word "dispensation?" How long does it take to count the number of times the word "relationship" is in the Bible?

All of these questions can be answered in seconds with a concordance. Without a concordance, you must reread large portions of scripture or the entire Bible to find these simple answers. A concordance of the Bible makes searching for words much easier by indexing every word alphabetically along with every verse where it is used.

Exhaustive concordances took years to create but are now widely available in print and in free Bible software. *Strong's Exhaustive Concordance* was first printed in 1890, just a few years after the car was invented. Today, most everyone has a car or uses one for transportation, but only a small percentage of people own a concordance. Perhaps this is why people are getting nowhere in Bible study.

If you want to move forward with your Bible study, learn to use a concordance. It has long been the most valuable tool to get ahead in Bible study. Bible study requires concordance work. Either you own a concordance, or you become one. It takes a lot of reading time to develop your own mental concordance. It takes three hours flipping burgers to get a concordance on Amazon for less than 20 dollars[1].

TIP #18: AVOID PROOF TEXTING

Proof texting is using Bible verses out of context to prove a point. It is a Bible study crime. It is most often committed while pushing a personal or political agenda. The harm in proof texting is that it substitutes the true meaning of God's words with personal opinion. Instead of asking, "What does God say," the proof texter asks, "Isn't there a verse somewhere in the Bible that supports me?"

The proof texter is looking for one verse to prove his point. If he does not find it in one translation, he will use

---

[1] Print concordances are translation specific. Make sure you get a KJV concordance or else it will not work with your Bible.

another. He is not concerned with what God says but in using God's authority to bolster his opinion.

Our opinions do not deserve the authority of God's words, especially his words taken out of context. Dispensational Bible study discourages proof texting. It requires we understand the context (historical, doctrinal, and spiritual) of a verse. Do not let someone proof text the Bible. Always seek the context of the verse references, and then rightly divide. Let God be true. Any criminal can be Biblical. It requires a student to be dispensational.

TIP #19: USE A DICTIONARY

You are never too old to use a dictionary. Outside of the Bible, it is one of the most important study tools you can own. Definitions of words get distorted. Look them up. A good dictionary of the language will supply you with the meaning, pronunciation, and perhaps etymological information. Look up related words or words in the definition to get further insight. Sometimes simple words like "walk" are read but never studied.

Many words have more than one definition. This requires you to look at the context. Many times when a pastor destroys your English Bible by saying, "The Greek word here means...," it is merely another definition of the same English word!

With an unabridged English dictionary you can gain the meaning of every word in your Bible without knowing Greek or Hebrew. I would suggest Webster's old 1828 at first, since it is dated closer to the words in the King James Bible.

Tip #20: The Bible, its Own Best Dictionary

Dictionaries record the meaning of words. They are useful in Bible study. However, the meanings of words in your Bible can change over time as less people use the Bible. For this reason, modern dictionaries sometimes can define Bible words incorrectly.

How can you guard against this? One way is to consult an older dictionary. A good popular recommendation is Noah Webster's Dictionary from 1828. It can be used or purchased online. From two centuries ago, this dictionary will contain definitions closer to those used in your King James Bible.

Some skeptics of your Bible will complain that the first English dictionaries were not produced until long after the King James Bible was translated. They are right. So how did people know what words meant without a dictionary? Answer: their usage in the context. The Bible is a big enough book that it can supply a definition to many words by comparing all the verses using the word.

To find the meaning (or meanings) of the word "oracle," we can collect all the verses that contain it and compare. We can find helpful meanings in verses such as 1 Kings 6:16, Acts 7:38, and Romans 3:2.

Modern dictionaries are better than no dictionary for Bible study. Older dictionaries are better at giving historical meanings, but the best dictionary is the Bible defining its own terms.

TIP #21: THE HISTORY OF WORDS

Knowing the history of words can help you understand the nature of their meanings. The study of the history of words is called etymology. A good etymological dictionary can reveal good information about how words evolved over time. With a Bible 400 years old, this can be useful.

Learning a new language is not necessary to dig deeper into a word if you have the history of the word in your own language.

If you do not have the money or resources to buy a shelf of etymological dictionaries, you can try this one: *www.etymonline.com*. It compiles etymologies from dozens of sources including those at Oxford and Cambridge. It will get you started.

It is from etymologies that we learn the word "gay" used in James 2:3 once meant something different from what is now familiar.

TIP #22: CHAPTERS AND VERSES

Chapter headings and verse numbers are not inspired. The system of chapters and verses in our Bibles was not widely adopted until the 16th century. The chapters and verses help us considerably when referencing and studying the Bible. However, if you are reading the Bible with the thought that the chapter headings are God's division of the material, you may be selling yourself short. Sometimes the thoughts of the previous chapter carry over into the next. Often a single verse does not equal a single sentence or thought. Sentences in the Bible are known to carry on for multiple verses. Better read the whole sentence to get the context.

The chapter and verse numbers are useful, but respect the text by reading the chapter before and after to get the context. Maybe the next verse has the answers to troubling passages, and only an uninspired chapter number keeps it separate. Do not let the numbers hinder your study.

TIP #23: APPRECIATE GENEALOGIES

Some of the most neglected passages of the Bible are genealogies. They are dry to read, lack the doctrinal depth of the epistles, have no narrative, and when put to song they make "Dem Bones" sound profound. Notwithstanding, genealogies serve many important purposes in the Bible. For example:

- They show divine inspiration and preservation by their accurate transmission through history.
- They authenticate people and places as part of real history and not myths and fables.
- They are used in prophecy to identify the Messiah (e.g., Son of David, Son of Abraham).
- They connect the first Adam and the last Adam proving that Christ died for all men.
- They show God's continual involvement and observation of history.
- Some genealogies are also chronologies that help to date events like creation, the flood, and the reign of David.

Throughout history, Bible believing men have spent years studying, comparing, and preserving the genealogies – and for good reason. They are the most important family records in history containing both the first man and the second man, the Lord from heaven (1 Cor 15:47).

Use them to create your own timeline of the Bible, and
you will find a better understanding of Bible history and
connections between books of the Bible. It is important to
know the place of genealogies: that they have been perfectly
preserved, and that they are profitable.

TIP #24:
TRUST THE BIBLE OVER RELIGIOUS CALENDARS

The study of chronology is a complex science that
includes precise calculations of days, times, months, and
years. Yet, with all their precision, calendars are still
influenced by religious tradition. Consider "Good Friday"
and "Easter Sunday," for example. Tradition says that Good
Friday is the day Jesus was crucified and that Easter Sunday
is the day Jesus resurrected.

However, the Bible says that Jesus was dead for three
days and three nights, explaining that he was dead for 72
hours (Matt 12:40). The 24-hour day theory affects more than
creation week. To make the Bible fit with the religious
calendar, this particular Saturday would need to be more
than 50 hours long! If you've been asking for more than 24
hours in a day, then this day is for you!

Either your Bible is right or the labels put on your
calendar by religious tradition are right. I choose the Bible
over tradition any day of the week (even so-called "holy
week"). The Bible is more trustworthy in its description of days
and times than any modern religious calendar. Thankfully, our
faith does not come from chronology and day observance.

Do not bother with religious calendars. Stick with the
Bible, which says Jesus was dead for three days but now is
raised from the dead for nearly two-thousand years.

TIP #25: STUDYING PROPHECY

When an apostle quotes a prophecy, it is good to have knowledge of the source to understand why it was referenced. Often only a small portion of the prophecy is quoted, and the meaning can be lost if we do not understand the prophecy in its original context.

When we reached Romans 9 in our book study of Romans, we found Paul quoting many prophecies concerning Israel and not the Church. That is why we went back to study Obadiah and Malachi verse-by-verse in preparation. Why Obadiah and Malachi? They are the key to understanding passages like Romans 9:13, which cause so many people to err in understanding salvation.

We must understand the prophets and Israel's program if we are ever going to see clearly the contrast to the mystery of Christ (Rom 16:25-26). Prophecy and mystery are different, but it is on the backdrop of prophecy that the mystery is manifest. All scripture is profitable. Study the prophets, and then rightly divide.

TIP #26: GOSPEL HARMONIES

Matthew, Mark, Luke, and John cover the same period of the Lord's ministry to Israel. Many of the same events are repeated. When people do not understand or respect the differences in these books, they try to combine them into a single telling. After all, why read something four times when you can read through it only once in a single gospel harmony, right?

This type of gospel harmonizing has multiple problems.

- Some events happened more than once, and harmonization often confuses them as the same event.
- The four books give a different perspective to similar events; you miss these dimensions when you combine them.
- John is not written as historical narrative, but as a proof that Jesus is the Son of God (John 20:31). Harmonization will always change the function of John.
- Each book has a unique tone/purpose/theme, and these are lost when they are all smashed together.
- God inspired four different books, not just one.

Gospel harmonies are a popular and subtle way to change the Bible. They are interesting as novelty but not useful for Bible study. Too much is missing or just does not make sense. When you get the urge to harmonize these four books and mutilate your Bible, remember the whispered words of wisdom from the well known English theologian, Sir McCartney, and "Let it be." Do not combine what God has kept separate.

Tip #27: Beware of Trivial Bible Study

The purpose of Bible study is not to discover the trivia that no one else has yet to see. On the contrary, profitable Bible study requires spending time on the foundational doctrines of the gospel.

Every saint of God needs to be personally edified in the doctrines of the gospel, our purpose, life in Christ, and right division. Too often, these important doctrines are only given a superficial study and ignored in order to find some new trivial thing.

Studying for Bible trivia is different from doctrinal study that produces mature saints. If the basic doctrines are milk, and the advanced are meat, then trivia is sugary candy. They may be interesting but do nothing to nourish you.

TIP #28:
BEWARE OF SUPERSTITIOUS NUMEROLOGY

Counting the letters in my name creates the combination 6-6-7. This means I am one letter away from being the antichrist (Rev 13:18). Of course, this is pure bunkum and so are many other practices of so-called Bible numerologists. Bible numerologists are always trying to find deeper meaning to the scripture through some secret pattern, code, or statistical anomaly.

The purveyors of such ideas are typically looking for proof that the Bible is God's word by finding a divine numeric fingerprint. However, the evidence for the Bible's divine inspiration does not rely on hidden codes, patterns, or numbers. Some will say that numbers themselves have a special meaning. This allows a secret Bible interpretation to come from giving words new numeric meaning. This is not a practice worthy of Bible believers.

Be wary of those who attach special meaning to numbers. Their supposed meanings are speculative at best and superstitious at worst. Moreover, numerology distracts from understanding the plainly revealed doctrinal mysteries of God in scripture (1 Cor 4:1; Eph 1:9). Stop counting words in your Bible and start studying it.

Tip #29: Memorizing Scripture

Sometimes people ask me how to better memorize Bible verses. It is extremely important to know your Bible, and time memorizing verses is time well spent. When you memorize verses they will be in your mind as tools ready when you need them. However, just having tools does not mean you know how to use them. Memorization is easier when you use what you are trying to remember.

In my experience, as I spent more time studying passages to understand the doctrines, an amazing thing happened. I began to memorize verses or parts of verses without even trying. I was thinking so much about the words of a passage to understand them in their context that my mind would automatically recall them.

The same goes for books of the Bible. You naturally remember where the most used books of the Bible are. Try finding Habakkuk – your memory will fail you. It is just not used very often, and if you do not use it, you lose it.

New-language learners testify that the best way to memorize new words is to use them in conversations. Perhaps the reason why you have trouble remembering verses is that you do not use them very often. Bible understanding is much better than Bible recitation. Memorizing Bible verses is profitable but only if you are going to use them. Otherwise, it may be a waste of time. Spend time reading and studying, then memorization will come naturally.

Tip #30: We All Need Daily Bible Reading

There is no substitute for the Bible. People who are seeking comfort, encouragement, or motivation do not find it in systematic theologies. People who are seeking sound doctrinal explanation do not find it in daily devotionals or counseling sessions. Daily reading in the Bible will guard you from becoming the cold hearted thinker void of compassion and usefulness. It will also protect you from being ignorant of doctrine while performing the ministry.

The Bible contains both doctrine and motivation, what some call teaching and preaching. It contains everything the believer needs to be an educated minister. There are too many ministers ignorant of Bible doctrine and too many educators lacking motivation to do real ministry work. Both find what they need in the same book.

Tip #31: Mindless Bible Reading

"Intellectual laziness lies at the bottom of a large percent of fruitless Bible reading." – Reuben Archer Torrey

Reuben was right. The Bible only brings profit when our brains are turned on. If reading the Bible is mindless or done as we are drifting off to sleep, then we might as well be reading the phone book and use the Bible as a paperweight or for pressing flowers.

It takes work to make money. It takes work to mine gold. It takes work to refine silver. What makes us think that the hidden treasures of wisdom and knowledge will be any easier to obtain. It takes work to dig them out. When they are found out, we can enjoy them forever.

"I rejoice at thy word, as one that findeth great spoil."
— Psalm 119:162

Mindlessly reading the Bible is like randomly walking around the earth hoping gold will be laying on the surface or trying to earn a living with money found lying in the street.

An ounce of quality beats a pound of quantity. Improve the quality of your Bible reading by thinking about a verse. Then, compare it to another. Repeat. This is dirty work, but it will bring profitable results if done regularly.

TIP #32: BE A BIBLE SHARPSHOOTER

The Bible says we are at war. Our wars are spiritual and doctrinal, not flesh and blood. We fight for power over men's souls and minds. We fight against every thing that exalts itself against the knowledge of God (2 Cor 10:3-5). Our weapon is the word of God (Eph 6:17). Words can strike the heart of our target: souls and minds. To shoot we must speak the words. To be accurate we must speak the right words. When the Bible is used without training or discernment, harm can be done and the battle lost.

When we learn to rightly divide the word of God, we become sharpshooters. Christianity has a lot of big guns and stockpiles of ammunition that miss the mark. Often we shoot ourselves in the foot. We do not need bigger guns; we need more sharpshooters.

TIP #33: ASK, "WHY?"

Before you study the Bible, pray. Before you pray, ask, "Why do I study the Bible?" It is easy to go through the motions of Bible study without the proper motivation. Doing something with desire will make your study more effective. You will see things you would not otherwise. Prayer can generate desire as you remind yourself and tell God why you study his words every day.

You can use this same technique in other areas of your life that become routine: work, cleaning, exercising, education. Ask yourself, "Why?" and remember:

> "Whether therefore ye eat, or drink, or whatsoever ye do, do all to the glory of God."   – 1 Corinthians 10:31

CONCLUSION

Dispensational right division is the key to understanding the Bible. Taking God's words literally without rightly dividing ends in failure, Bible mistakes, and doctrinal confusion. Failing to take the Bible literally leaves us only with doubts about whether God truly inspired the Bible and can actually say what he means. God forbid!

The only way to let God be true, possess a Bible without error, and take it literally is to start rightly dividing.

ADDITIONAL STUDY RESOURCES

Grace Ambassadors

Hundreds of free lessons from the Bible rightly divided with charts, video, audio, and verse-by-verse commentary. Subscribe online to get more Bible study tips like the ones in this book.

GraceAmbassadors.com

The Grace Hymnal

This mid-Acts dispensational hymnal represents an unprecedented collection of original, revised, and entirely rewritten songs that teach the Bible rightly divided.

GraceHymnal.com

A Dispensational Chart

Make sense of your Bible with this four-panel chart that shows God's progressive revelation as a colorful timeline.

DispensationalChart.com

Ambassadors Publishing

Publishing resources to advance dispensational Bible study and the preaching of Jesus Christ according to the revelation of the mystery.

AmbassadorsPublishing.com

CONTACT INFORMATION

Find more information and ask your questions about the gospel of Jesus Christ, mid-Acts Pauline dispensational right division, King James Bible believing, and the revelation of the mystery at:

Grace Ambassadors Bible Fellowship
6281 S 900 W
Swayzee, Indiana 46986
www.GraceAmbassadors.com

For more information about this book, to order more copies, or request a free catalog, contact:

P.O. Box 161,
Swayzee, Indiana 46986
www.AmbassadorsPublishing.com